MW00886042

Philippians

Finding Fullness of Joy in the Circumstances of Life

Sheryl Pellatiro

For more information on other resources available, and ministry opportunities, please visit our website at:

www.solidtruthministries.com

Copyright © 2018 Sheryl Pellatiro. All rights reserved.
No part of this publication may be reproduced or
transmitted in any form or by any means, electronic
or mechanical, including photocopying, recording, or any
information storage and retrieval system, without
permission in writing from the author.

Unless otherwise noted, all Scripture quotations are
from the Holy Bible; New International Version®,
Copyright© 1973, 1978, 1984 by
International Bible Society.

The "NIV" and "New International Version" trademarks
are registered in the United States Patent and Trademark
office by International Bible Society.

ISBN – 1723447358
ISBN – 978-1723447358

Contact Information:

Solid Truth Ministries, Inc.
www.solidtruthministries.com
www.sherylpellatiro.com
sheryl@solidtruthministries.com

Rejoice in the Lord always. I will say it again: Rejoice!

Philippians 4:4

Dedicated to…

Elsie, Betty, Rommy, Lisa-Marie, Martha, Naomi, Kathy,
Jill, Cathy, and so many more who have
supported me through partnership, encouragement, affirmation,
edits, and endorsements. I'm the one truly blessed
to have so many faithful ones in my life.
Thank you.

The Church at Philippi. Thank you for your steadfast
faithfulness and partnership with the apostle Paul. You
have shown us how to keep on keeping on
for the kingdom of God.

All those who want to know Christ more. I pray this
Bible study will give you rich insight into
the heart of God. Because of you, I research and write
with joy and gladness.

Table of Contents

Introduction

Negativity is all around us. We find it in our communities, in our work places, in our schools, on television, and on social media. Negativity can turn a tender heart into a heart of stone and cause anger, resentment, and disillusionment. Occasionally, the news focuses on positive things happening, but most of the time it's negative. And scary! Negativity, along with the circumstances of life, can spiral us into a dark place. Hence, the dreariness of life will hinder us from living with an abundant joy.

Here's the good news though: joy is a special gift Jesus came to give us. Joy is different than happiness because happiness is fleeting and is based on the happenings – or the good circumstances – in our life. Therefore, we can't always be happy. But we *can* be joyful no matter what's going on. We long for joy. We pray for inner contentment. Most of us have known it at one time, but maybe it has eluded us. And we wonder if we'll ever know it again. With that said, there's not a better book of the Bible than Philippians to show us that joy *is* possible.

The apostle Paul lived in a negative world and his circumstances were sometimes daunting. At the writing of this letter, Paul was in prison in Rome, where he was free to minister, but not free to travel. He was confined in a city hostile to the gospel. Yet, he was filled with joy. Paul wanted the believers in Philippi to experience the same kind of joy he knew despite the difficulties they faced. So, he wrote this letter to tell them how they could attain inner joy no matter what struggles they were going through.

Paul founded the church at Philippi on his second missionary journey. Many years later, as he neared the end of his life, Paul wrote a letter to this group of believers he had grown to love. One of the main reasons for Paul's letter was to express his appreciation and affection for the Philippian believers. We learn that this church - more than any other church – supported Paul in his ministry through prayers, gifts, and money. He shared a special bond and a great fellowship with this congregation. But what the Philippian believers gained from this letter was far more valuable than gold and would sustain them in the good times and the bad times. What was that? Their beloved teacher would teach them how to have fullness of joy.

Everyone needs to study Philippians. We live in a different time and we're immersed in a different culture, but we still struggle as they did. Philippi was a Roman colony governed by Roman laws and subject to Roman rule. Nero was emperor of Rome and hated Christians. No doubt, the believers in the church at Philippi were living in fear as they heard about Christians being imprisoned and savagely killed. Paul surely heard about their dilemma and wrote to encourage them in their faith and to help them find joy in the midst of it all.

We are also immersed in a dark world surrounded by evil and chaos. It's easy to be consumed by worry, anxiety, and fear. But here's the thing: fear and joy cannot dwell together in our hearts. God wants us to experience fullness of joy, so He offered us this incredible letter Paul penned centuries ago. If we are careful to apply the principles in this book, I'm sure we will emerge on the other side with more joy and less anxiety. The next six weeks should offer us great insight into the brightened world of joy – a place where every Christian should live.

Week 1
Paul and the Beloved Philippians

Day 1
The Beginnings
Day 2
Salutation and Gratitude
Day 3
Praying for the Saints
Day 4
Advancement of the Gospel
Day 5
Every Way

We have our favorite Bible characters. We love Moses the servant, Joshua the warrior, David the worshiper, Ruth the devoted, Hannah the humble one, Rahab the believer, Peter the impetuous, and Stephen the fearless apostle. They inspire us in our own quest to be more like Christ. But for some people, believe it or not, the apostle Paul doesn't make their favorite list. He seems a little rough around the edges and a bit callous at times. Perhaps they're somewhat intimated by his strong personality and debating skills. But let's remember that most of Paul's writings were to address problems in the church, in addition to teaching solid doctrine.

The book of Philippians will show us another side of the apostle Paul. I believe his letter to this church will reveal a softer, gentler side. This church held a special place in Paul's heart and his affection for them is disclosed through every passage. He writes: **"I thank my God every time I remember you" (Philippians 1:3)**.

I have a few amazing women who have been my number one cheerleaders. They stand beside me in everything I do, clapping and cheering me on. Oh, how I appreciate them. Well, the apostle Paul had his grandest supporters as well: the Philippian church. No wonder he smiled and thanked God every time he thought of them. Our lesson this week will give us great insight into this affectionate relationship Paul shared with the Philippians. And here's something to keep in mind as we study: every intricate part of this book is dripping with *joy*.

Day 1
The Beginnings

Joyous Jewel
About midnight Paul and Silas were praying and singing hymns to God, and the other prisoners were listening to them. Acts 16:25

Author and Christian evangelical leader John Stott said, *"Every Christian should be both conservative and radical; conservative in preserving the faith and radical in applying it."* [1] These words surely describe the apostle Paul. From the moment he was profoundly transformed **(Acts 9:1-9)**, he committed himself to the cause of the Gospel. He lived with a fierce resolve. He defended what God entrusted to him and lived wholly to bring the Good News to the world. Paul surely poured himself out to carry the mission of Jesus to the world.

In the weeks ahead, we will be inspired by Paul's spirited passion as he ministered to one specific church. But before we dive into the letter, we need to first examine the beginnings of this church. Gaining a little background is always helpful as we move forward.

The church at Philippi was founded by Paul on his second missionary journey. Begin by reading **Acts 16:1-12**, and then look at the map and trace Paul's journey.

Paul's 2nd Missionary Journey

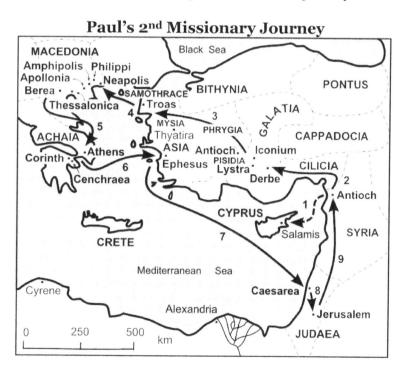

How did Paul end up in Philippi (Macedonia) **(Acts 16:9)**?

How did Paul respond to this vision **(Acts 16:10)**?

Acts is often called "the acts of the apostles." But I think a better title would be "the acts of the Holy Spirit." This passage clearly shows that the Holy Spirit was intimately involved in the actions and decisions of the apostles. This is called *divine sovereignty*. In this case, God was dominating Paul's movements. At the outset, Paul may have been discouraged because he truly believed he was to go north into Asia. But God re-routed him. And Paul obeyed.

What does **Proverbs 16:9** say about divine sovereignty? Have you seen this at work in your life? What do these words mean to you in relation to your ministry right now?

If the apostles were not clear on God's path, then we may not always be either. When God changes our plans or redirects our steps, it's for His purposes. But when that happens, we may feel like we failed God. Believing we're a failure can lead to discouragement and thoughts of wanting to quit. So, let Paul's experience encourage you to follow the Holy Spirit's leading. Always be flexible because He may just redirect your steps. But it *will* be for the greater good, no doubt, as we'll see in Paul's situation.

Now, read **Acts 16:13-15** and give a summary.

I love Paul's determination to fulfill God's Great Commission and the call on his life - **"to carry [God's] name before the Gentiles and their kings and before the people of Israel" (Acts 9:15)**. The first order of business on any given missionary trip was to find the synagogue in town – the place where Jewish people would be gathered for instruction and worship. But there wasn't a synagogue in Philippi. So in the absence of a synagogue, places of prayer were often set up. In Philippi, the place of prayer was outside of town in an open space and by a river, so the people could use the water for purification rites. When Paul arrived, he found a group of women gathered.

Review **Acts 16:14-15**. Who was the first convert to Christianity?

What happened then?

It was a man's world in that culture, but throughout the Bible we find that women often played a specific role in God's redemptive purposes. Here are a few examples: *Ruth* (the foreigner) and *Rahab* (the prostitute) were listed in Jesus' genealogy; *Esther* saved Israel from annihilation; *Hannah* gave birth to the prophet Samuel; *Deborah* was a prophet and a judge over Israel; *Elizabeth* raised John the Baptist – the forerunner to Jesus; *Mary* was chosen to bear the Christ child; *Priscilla*, along with her husband Aquila, served with Paul. And in our story, *Lydia* became the first convert to Christianity in Philippi.

As you observe Lydia's actions, how do you know she was instantly transformed?

Relate **2 Corinthians 5:17** to Lydia. How do you see this truth evident in her reaction?

A fire has started. The Holy Spirit has begun to command attention in this prominent Roman city. The women are sensing a powerful movement and their hearts are bursting with excitement. But you and I know that whenever good things are happening, evil is hiding in the shadows just waiting. Waiting for the perfect opportunity to rear its ugly head.

Let's continue in our story and see what happens next. Read **Acts 16:16-34** and summarize. Ask the Holy Spirit to quicken your heart as you read this story.

Joy in the book of Philippians can be traced all the way back to this day when the gospel made its entrance into this city and shook things up, starting by the river and concluding in a jail cell. One of the most awesome ways to finding fullness of joy is through worship, offering praise to the One who deserves it all, even when things are not going so well.

A dark and dreary place on this night was turned into a ray of light. Renowned pastor, Skip Heitzig, quotes missionary and theologian, E. Stanley Jones, as saying: *"When I first met Jesus Christ, I felt I swallowed sunshine."* I wonder if the guard and the other prisoners felt the same way. Heaven converged upon this stinky place of confinement and opened the sweet-smelling gates of freedom as songs of praise were lifted into the heavenly realms. The prisoners listened. And then the unbelievable happened – the prison doors flew open.

Paul and Silas show us exactly how we should respond when circumstances are not favorable, or even when they're horrible. They were severely beaten, humiliated, thrown into a dark dungeon, and shackled at the ankles. They needed a hospital bed, not a dirty musty cell. But instead of shaking their fist at God, they worshiped Him.

What are your difficult struggles right now? Write them down.

Do you need to change how you're responding in the midst of your difficulties? How?

In relation to your struggles, what does God tell you from the following verses?

Deuteronomy 31:8:

Psalm 46:1:

Psalm 23:4:

Based on our story at hand, here's what God is saying to me… Being in God's will is not always comfortable, but it does offer us courage. God can turn any bad situation into something amazing. Complaining gives Satan the upper hand, but worship moves the hand of God. Every opportunity can be used to bring glory to God.

What is God speaking to you about right now? Ponder this question before answering.

I wish we had more time to study the early days in Philippi, but we will close our lesson today with a final scene. According to **Acts 16:40**, where did Paul and Silas go after they left the prison, and who did they find there?

Remember, this is just a couple days after Lydia was saved by the river. Did you notice there were other believers in the house? Wow, that was fast. Something tells me that Lydia went right to work telling people what happened to her. I wonder if the enthusiasm just came spilling out as she recalled how in an instant she was changed.

I would say this church got off to a great start. And God used some very unfortunate circumstances to grow the Philippian church as well. In just a matter of days, Lydia (and her converts), the jail guard (and his household), and probably many of the prisoners were the founding members of the church. Paul would grow to love this place and these people.

As we move forward, put yourself in the shoes of these believers. What do you want God to do in your life through this study? Do you need more joy? More contentment? More peace? Deeper love? More biblical insight? Write down what you need and then write out your prayer.

Through each lesson in our study, we'll draw out principles to help us find fuller joy. Ponder each one and then find the place where you can write them down at the back of the book. Now ponder today's *Finding Fullness of Joy* principle and then write it at the back of the book.

Finding Fullness of Joy
Worshiping God in the good and the bad

Day 2
Salutation and Gratitude

Joyous Jewel

Being confident of this, that he who began a good work in you will carry it on to completion until the day of Christ Jesus. Philippians 1:6

I'm drawn to joyful people. Their passion inspires me. I want to have such joy that people say, "I gotta get me some of what she's got." The good news is that Jesus has mapped out a pathway for us to be *filled* with joy.

We now begin with Paul's letter to the Church at Philippi. Read **Philippians 1:1-8** and write down the key components.

Paul begins with a salutation **(1:1-2)**. Answer the following questions:

What does the author tell you about himself?

Who was he writing to? What information does he disclose about his recipients?

The apostle Paul wrote the letter and Timothy was the one who would deliver it to the church **(Philippians 2:19)**. At the writing of this letter, Timothy was helping Paul in his ministry.

Observing the salutation, what title did Paul give to himself and to Timothy **(Philippians 1:1)**?

Some translations use the word *bond-servant*, which seems to be a better rendering. It comes from the Greek word, *doulos*, and means "one who is subservient, and entirely at the disposal of his master." In Roman times, the term bond-servant could refer to someone who *voluntarily* served others. [2] Throughout the New Testament, the word bond-servant is applied metaphorically to someone absolutely devoted to Jesus. In his devotional, *My Utmost for His Highest*, Oswald Chambers describes a bond-servant like this: *"It means the breaking of my independence with my own hand and surrendering to the supremacy of the Lord Jesus. No one can do this for me, I must do it myself."* [3] Powerful words, don't you agree?

Paul could have identified himself as a preacher, teacher, evangelist, writer, or apostle (as in other letters). All of these applied and were worthy titles. Instead, he called himself a bond-servant. What does this tell you about Paul?

Relate **Matthew 16:24** to being a bond-servant. Will you answer Jesus' call? How will you live?

In the salutation of this letter, we learn that Paul is writing to the people in the church at Philippi – believers. And Paul gives them a sneak peek into what it means to be a child of God. Write out your own definitions to these features:

Holy people:

Belong to Jesus Christ:

These aspects to Christianity are true of *every* believer. In that case, how do these things influence your life as a Christian?

According to **Philippians 1:2**, what two components are the by-products of being a Christian?

Paul often opens and closes his letters with the words *grace* and *peace*. And always in this order. You see, peace is *only* possible in Jesus and *only* by grace. Many people are searching for peace, but they'll never find it apart from Jesus. Aren't you thankful you know Him?

Now, let's move forward with the remainder of our passage. Such good stuff! Read again **Philippians 1:3-8**. How did Paul feel about the believers in Philippi and why?

Do you remember what we learned about Paul's experience in Philippi on his first visit? Paul experienced some truly awesome things, but he also encountered some unbelievably awful things. Review Day 1 and recap what some of those awful things were.

Now listen carefully to what I'm about to say because it may just set you on a pathway to joy. Like Paul, we all have those not-so-good memories. It could be a certain time in your life, a church, a ministry, a job, a relationship, or a situation. And when you think of that time, you only see the terrible things that happened. All the good is clouded over by all the bad memories.

What happened to the apostle Paul in Philippi was horrific, a day he surely would have loved to forget. But there was a church in that town – a church with some amazing people. People who loved him. And God was at work in that city. The Gospel was being proclaimed. The church at Philippi was a beacon of light on a hillside. And that's what Paul focused on. Somehow, he was able to push aside all the bad stuff and think about the work God was doing. And this brought such joy to the apostle's heart.

So here's the moral of the story: when we can look beyond the bad and rejoice at what God is doing, then joy replaces bitterness and sadness. I had some really bad things happen to me in a workplace. In fact, it was at a church. But God also used that experience to draw me closer to Him and to teach me patience and trust. God worked in my life tremendously. And He was doing some fabulous things in that church. In the beginning I struggled with negative thoughts. But then God helped me to put away the bad thoughts. Eventually, the good stuff emerged.

This might be a good time for an evaluation. Is there something in your life that you only see the bad? And because of that, you're consumed by bitterness or pain. Write down what it is and then write out your prayer to God asking for deliverance.

Let's now look at why Paul felt such strong affection for this church.

They were…

1. Partners in spreading the Gospel (1:5)!

The word *partnership* comes from the Greek word *koinonia* and is most commonly translated "fellowship." It can also mean "the close association between persons emphasizing what is common between them. [4] The latter definition is a better rendering for our context.

It must have been so comforting for the apostle Paul to know that this church continued the work that began when Lydia and the others accepted his message and received Christ. Many of the churches operating in the first century were struggling to stay afloat because of unresolved issues within the body. Not this church. Oh, how thankful Paul was.

According to **Romans 1:16-17**, why should we spread the Gospel?

The Gospel is *good news*, not bad news. It's the only way for salvation. And God works through the Gospel. Someone, like Paul, shared it with you and the moment you received it as your own, your life was changed forever. Those who shared it were partnering with Paul and the early believers. If the Philippian partnership caused Paul to rejoice, imagine how God must be so pleased when we choose to partner with others in spreading the Gospel.

Look up **Ephesians 4:16**. What is expected of us as members of the body of Christ? How does our partnership benefit the whole body, the Church?

Once the work of God begins in us, how long does it last **(Philippians 1:6)**?

2. Sharers in his *imprisonment* (1:7)!

In addition to the money and the gifts the church sent to Paul **(Philippians 4:15-19)**, they were genuinely concerned for his welfare **(Philippians 4:10)**. No doubt, they prayed for him unceasingly. And for some, they also shared in his suffering.

3. Sharers in *defending* and *confirming* the truth the Gospel (1:7)!

The word for *defend* means, "to answer." What is the mandate in **1 Peter 3:15**?

A defense attorney is someone who stands up for his clients; supporting them through powerful persuasive words and thought-out responses. A true believer is someone who will defend the Gospel. They will stand up for it no matter the cost. When people try to dismantle it with words or actions, believers should not stand back and let them destroy the *only* thing that can change people's lives and the *only* thing that offers eternal security.

To *confirm* something means to "establish accuracy, validity, or genuineness." Our defense of the Gospel confirms its accuracy and validity. The early believers risked their very lives for this message. That alone was a confirmation of its genuineness. I've heard it called the *unadulterated* Word of God. There are NO errors. And when we placed our faith in Jesus Christ, we believed it. That belief should be so strong in us that we partner with Paul and the Philippian believers in defending and confirming the Gospel.

Are you right now defending and confirming the Gospel? If you've been a little lax in that area, what can you do to partner with the early believers?

Paul was filled with joy at the thought of the Philippians. I hope you gained a wealth of valuable insight you can apply to your life. Don't forget to ponder our *Finding Fullness of Joy* principle below and then write it at the back of the book.

Finding Fullness of Joy

Looking beyond the bad and recognizing the work God is doing

Praying for the Saints

Joyous Jewel

I pray that your love will overflow more and more, and that you will keep on growing in knowledge and understanding. Philippians 1:9

This morning I was reading about leaders in a large church who are involved with occultist material. This church reaches thousands on a weekend. Then I was reminded of what Jesus said about the end days: **"Many will come in my name, claiming, 'I am the Christ.' They will deceive many... And many false prophets will appear and deceive many people" (Matthew 24:5, 11).**

The problem we're seeing in the Church today is that people are drifting from the standard of Scripture and going outside of its boundaries in search of spiritual awareness. There are many prominent preachers and teachers leading people to a place that is not of God. Here's what we need to always remember: God has spoken through His Word and everything we need to know about the way God works, how to live, what to believe, and information about the future, is written in His Word. So the best and safest place for us to be is immersed in the *inspired* Word of God. A plumb-line is a measuring tool of a structure, and God's Word is heaven's measuring tool of spiritual awareness.

The apostle Paul spent considerable time addressing this issue in his letter to the Galatian church as they were being influenced by wrong teaching coming in from the outside.

What did Paul say to the Church at Galatia in **Galatians 1:6-7**?

The best way to stay solid in your beliefs and to not drift like so many have already done, is to strive for maturity in Christ. The apostle Paul encouraged his readers to **"grow to maturity" (2 Corinthians 13:11 NLT).**

Look up **Ephesians 4:14-15** and compare immaturity with maturity. What are the features of both?

Immaturity	*Maturity*

Summarize why we should seek to become mature in our faith.

Not only did Paul speak about maturity; he also prayed for it. Paul wasn't just a preacher, leader, church founder, and apostle; he was also a *prayer warrior*. In fact, he was a *devoted* prayer. Let's look at this in the letter he penned to the Church at Philippi.

Read **Philippians 1:9-11** and write down the key things Paul prayed for.

If we could sum up Paul's prayer with one word, we might call it *maturity*. Paul knew that while the Philippian church was strong and solid, he also knew they could easily falter if they didn't grow to become mature believers. In this prayer, Paul affirms four marks of Christian maturity. Spend quality time on each of them.

Paul prayed that they would be…

1. **Full of love (Philippians 1:9)!**

Being full of love is a sure sign of Christian maturity. The Greek word for *love* in this passage is *agape*, the highest form of love in the Bible. It's selfless, sacrificial, and unconditional. It's the kind of love Jesus had for His Father and for His followers. It's the kind of love we are supposed to have toward believers *and* non-believers.

This love extends far beyond emotions – it's much more than a feeling, sentiment, or just saying the words, "I love you." Agape love is demonstrated through actions. This is surely the kind of love people are drawn to. Since we are lights in this world, we are to demonstrate agape love.

The Bible is filled with passages on how we are to [agape] love others. Read the following verses and write down how we are to love:

John 15:12-13:

Romans 12:9:

Romans 13:10:

Ephesians 4:2:

Ephesians 5:2:

How can we love this way? How can we love the way Jesus loved? Well, it's *humanly* impossible. But because Jesus' full love has been poured out in us, we can pour out His love into others. It's not always easy, but it *is* possible to love this way. Imagine the witness we will become if we strive for mature love.

What is God speaking to you about right now? What is your plan of action?

Paul prayed that they would be...

2. Forever growing (Philippians 1:9)!

According to Paul's prayer, there are two things we should seek to grow in:

- Knowledge

The word *knowledge* comes from the Greek word *epignosis.* This is a compound word: *epi* (upon) and *gnosis* (knowledge); hence, upon-knowledge, or more specifically, "detailed knowledge." This compound word appears sixty-two times in the New Testament.

What are we to grow in our knowledge of, according to the following verses?

Ephesians 1:17:

Ephesians 4:13:

We might sum it up by saying that Paul prayed the Philippian believers would continue to grow in their knowledge of Christ, the Christ of Scripture. It's important we learn the doctrine of the Bible. What does Paul teach about God? Jesus? Salvation? Scripture? Oh, how important solid biblical teaching is. It's not enough to just go to church on Sundays and serve in your local body. We need to keep on growing in rich biblical doctrine.

- Understanding

Knowledge won't help us unless we understand it. It's always good to expand your study of God's Word by using commentaries, books, and reading articles. Of course, it's important to make sure the teachers and authors are reputable sources. *In the back of the book, I've listed some of my favorite biblical resources.*

Paul prayed that they would be...

3. Filled with discernment (Philippians 1:10)!

Paul prays that they will discern what really matters. In other words, they will sift through the wrong ideas to find what is right. We often get off track with this one, but Paul plainly tells us what really matters.

- **To live pure and blameless lives.**

This is usually the furthest thing from the Christian mindset. The word *pure* is defined as *sincere* in the King James Version translation. Our English word *sincere* comes from a Latin word that means "unadulterated, pure, unmixed." In ancient times merchants would often patch cracked porcelain with wax. A merchant who wanted his customers to be assured of his integrity would advertise his porcelain as "without wax." [5] Paul's desire for the Philippians is that they would be "without wax," pure and blameless in their conduct.

What does this mean to you, and why do you think Paul wanted this for the believers?

Paul prayed that they would be…

4. **Fruitful in Christian Service (Philippians 1:11)!**

Write down what Paul is referring to in **Philippians 1:11**.

We often think of Christian service as the "church activities" we do. But I believe Paul's prayer clearly reveals that it's more important for us to produce the kind of spiritual fruit that comes when we are in fellowship with Christ.

What does **John 15:4** say about bearing fruit?

Here's what's important: we cannot produce spiritual fruit **(Galatians 5:22-23)** apart from Christ. We need to strive for intimacy with the One who produces godly fruit in us.

Lastly, what does this fruit result in **(Philippians 1:11)**?

Paul surely demonstrated how important it is to pray for our brothers and sisters in Christ. Review today's lesson and write down one feature you've decide to work on. And then ponder today's *Finding Fullness of Joy* principle before writing it down in the back of the book.

Finding Fullness of Joy

Praying for the growth and understanding in others

Day 4
Advancement of the Gospel

Joyous Jewel

Now I want you to know, brothers, that what has happened to me has really served to advance the gospel. Philippians 1:12

Begin by reading **Philippians 1:12-14** and summarize.

We will divide this passage into three words: Passion, Prison, Proclamation.

- **Passion!**

Summarize the following verses and then post your answers to the questions on the lines below.

Romans 1:9:

1 Corinthians 9:16:

1 Corinthians 9:23:

What was Paul's passion? _____

How do you know it was his passion? _____

We read in **Acts 9:1**: **"Meanwhile, Saul was still breathing out murderous threats against the Lord's disciples. He went to the high priest and asked him for letters to the synagogues in Damascus, so that if he found any there who belonged to the Way, whether men or women, he might take them as prisoners to Jerusalem."** In that day, Saul was a scary force to be reckoned with. Without a doubt, the believers in Damascus were shivering in fear when they heard the murderous Pharisee was on his way to their city. But as Paul approached Damascus, something supernatural happened. A light from heaven pierced through the darkest part of his soul as he heard Jesus' voice speak to him **(Acts 9:3-4)**. He fell to the ground and was instantly transformed. A new creature!

21

There's nothing that fuels a passionate soul more than a changed life. From the onset, Paul was filled with *passion* **(Acts 9:20)**. And according to Scripture, we can surely sum up Paul's passion with two words: *The Gospel*. In all of Paul's writings, he mentions the Gospel some 70-80 times. Hence, he was driven by the message that changed his life. He devoted his life to share this message to the world, no matter where he was, what he was doing, or what his circumstances were.

From the beginning of his ministry, Paul was on mission with God. And throughout the rest of his life, he never gave up, never stopped – not even when he was in prison. In fact, prison life propelled his passion even more. Nothing kept him from speaking the Gospel into the hearts of people. Don't you wish you could have been in his presence at least once? Something tells me that we would be mesmerized by the powerful and passionate words coming from Paul's lips.

Are you on mission with God? If so, on what mission are you partnering with God? How are you living it out?

Are you passionate? If so, describe this passion. If not, what will you do to become more passionate?

- **Prison!**

Let's begin with a brief background on Paul's Roman days in prison, the time in which the book of Philippians was written. Read the following passage and write down what you learn about those days.

Acts 28:16-31:

The apostle Paul had been highly persecuted everywhere he went, so this time in Rome must have been a reprieve from that. Rather than a dirty dungeon cell, he was given his own rented house for two years. While he couldn't travel, he could receive visitors. And many came to see him. The praetorium guard was the elite of Roman soldiers. Every few hours a new guard was brought in and chained by the wrist to the apostle Paul.

Again, what did Paul do during these two years **(Acts 28:30-31)**?

I wonder how much sleep Paul got. Maybe a catnap every now and then. He had a mission and he would move in it no matter what. Day and night, he proclaimed the Gospel message. The guards were chained to him, so they listened. They had nowhere to go, nowhere to hide. The message of the resurrection of Jesus Christ was unlike any message they had ever heard. After being chained to Paul several hours a day, imagine the conversation at the dinner table with their families. *This is what he said today! He makes a lot of sense! He's almost convinced me!*

The place of Paul's confinement became his commission. He didn't sit around and play solitaire all day waiting for his release and the opportunity to travel again. No! He ministered to those who came to see him, he shared the Gospel with those without Christ, he prayed for the saints, and he honored God by his faithfulness.

Paul's confinement served as a catalyst to mobilize the Gospel to the ends of the earth. I've spent most of my adult life teaching God's Word. But there was a time I felt confined by limited opportunities to use my creative gifts of writing Bible studies. I believed that the Bible studies would never reach the multitudes without a publisher's backing. After many rejections by publishing houses, I felt defeated and contemplated quitting. Then I began to see the opportunities for online communities of believers. I knew God was calling me to use this venue to proclaim truth.

Several years ago, God opened the door for my first online Bible study. I also found that having a publisher's backing didn't matter to most of my Bible students. If God's fingerprint and His anointing are on the studies, then He will use them to change people's lives. And that's exactly what has happened. Like Paul, my confinement caused me to branch out into a different venue – a venue I would have never considered. I'm glad I didn't quit.

Let me ask you…

Do you feel confined? Stuck? Maybe in a job you don't like? Perhaps in a difficult relationship? Or in an unforeseen circumstance? Do you feel restricted by the people in your life? Limited in opportunities to use your gifts? Here's an assignment: Write down what you feel confined in, and then write out how you can change it for the good of the Kingdom. Paul should serve as an example for all of us.

- **Proclamation!**

While Paul was in prison, the message of the Gospel spread like wildfire. The sequence went something like this: little rented home → into the streets → into communities → into Roman homes → and into Caesar's palace. No wonder Paul said that **"what has happened to me has really served to advance the gospel" (Philippians 1:12)**.

According to the following verses, what was the result of Paul's confinement?

Acts 28:23-24, 30-31:

Philippians 1:12:

Philippians 1:13-14:

I can hear it now: *Well, since Paul is in prison and unable to travel and preach, we must carry on his work. We must proclaim the Gospel message.* Hence, the Gospel advanced even more in Paul's absence, his confinement. How awesome is that?

Let's look at one more glorious result to Paul's imprisonment. What was it, according to **Philippians 4:21-22**?

Imagine a rough-around-the-edges, raggedy-clothed servant of the Lord sitting next to a clean-shaven, heavily-armed Roman soldier having a Bible study and praying together. There was a time that Paul despised the Romans. Now look at them. Oh, how the heavens must have rejoiced at such a sight. There's nothing more powerful than a passionate sword bearer willing to wield it no matter the circumstances. All it takes is a little passion and a strong commitment to be on mission with Jesus.

Will you allow God to turn your circumstances into something He can use? Write out your prayer.

Here's one final amazing thing about Paul's Roman imprisonment. Not only did Paul preach the Gospel with his lips, but he also wrote four letters – Ephesians, Philippians, Colossians and Philemon – with his hands. These four books have been labeled by the church as the "prison epistles." So during Paul's time in prison, there was a *great* advancement of the Gospel, and a *great* strengthening in the church.

I say, Halleluiah!

What is God speaking to you about today? Write out your thoughts.

Now, ponder our *Finding Fullness of Joy* principle and write it at the back of the book.

Finding Fullness of Joy

Using your confinement as an opportunity for Christ

Every Way

Joyous Jewel

But what does it matter? The important thing is that in every way, whether from false motives or true, Christ is preached. And because of this I rejoice. Philippians 1:18

Author, speaker, and quadriplegic, Joni Eareckson Tada said, "Believers are never told to *become* one; we already *are* one and are expected to act like it." [6] How true this is, but unfortunately, disunity – rather than unity – often dominates the body of Christ. This isn't just a 21ˢᵗ century problem in the Church but can be traced all the way back to the early Church. In fact, the New Testament writers devoted great amounts of time to writing about this existing problem in the Church.

Now before we go any further, you may be wondering why disunity has been a pervading problem in the Church when clearly the body should be functioning together to bring glory to God. The answer to this question can be summed up with one word – or should I say, one name: *Satan*. His playground is the Church. He nonchalantly meanders in the door specifically to look for ways to divide. He's smart! He knows that if the Church is divided, then it will fall. Here's something we need to know: God adds to the family, multiplies the family, and at times, subtracts from the family (remember Ananias and Sapphira in **Acts 5:1-12**?). But God *never* divides the family. That's Satan's doing.

Now read **Philippians 1:15-19** and summarize.

Paul's thoughts here in this passage are a continuation of the previous passage. Read **verse 14**. Now, would you say the troublemakers in **1:15-19** were Christians or non-Christians?

Without a doubt, Paul is talking about Christians – brothers in Christ. This may surprise you because when do Christians treat their fellow brothers and sisters with such contempt? Sadly, *all the time*. There are several different directions we could take with this passage, but it's important we learn how to handle situations like this when we face confliction. And trust me, those doing God's work will surely collide with opposing forces from time to time. In this passage, we observe two types of preachers: the ones that are anti-Paul and the ones that are pro-Paul. Let's begin with the ones that are anti-Paul first.

From our passage, fill in the blanks:

Vs. 15 - It is true that some preach Christ out of _____ and _____...

Vs. 17 - The former preach Christ out of _____ _____**, not sincerely, supposing that they can** _____ _____ _____ **for me while I am in chains.**

In short, Paul references four characteristics of the contentious people causing him trouble.

Envious	**Self-seekers**
Competitive	**Troublemakers**

I've listed them, with a short definition, below. Next to each one, write out why you think these people caused Paul grief.

Envious (feeling of displeasure produced by witnessing or hearing of the advantage or prosperity of others):

Competitive (argumentative, quarrelsome, causing discord):

Self-seekers (Out for self only):

Troublemakers (malicious):

The Church should be a healthy place, but unfortunately, it rarely is. Paul had his work cut out for him because he wrote most of his letters to address problems in the church. And these four things were gaining momentum. The apostle doesn't give specifics, but we can probably guess what some of the problems were and what their motives were in preaching the Gospel.

I'm guessing that these people were using Paul's confinement to boost their own selfish cause. They saw his predicament as an opportunity. The ones jealous of Paul's leadership success and the power in which he moved in Christ, sought praise from men. The argumentative ones just wanted to do better than Paul. And with Paul out of the picture (so to speak), the self-seeking ones saw this as an opportunity to make a name for themselves in the Christian community. Finally, some preached just to make Paul's troubles worse.

Obviously, there were many preaching with *wrong* motives. Have you seen people in your life act on impure motives? How about in the Church? Write down your experience. What was the result?

According to **Proverbs 16:2**, why are motives important?

Motives are what drive us. And it's vital we have pure motives for everything we do. We may be focused on what we're doing and how we're doing it but neglecting the motives behind it. So it's important we do a "motive" check right now. Go to God with the work you're doing and ask Him to reveal the motives of your heart.

The passage before us today – **Philippians 1:15-19** – is a powerful reminder of one important truth. Ponder it before moving forward...

The power is in the message, not the messenger!

Paul was a prime example of this. He was powerful in word and deed, yet he showed his audience a different side. What message did Paul convey in **1 Corinthians 2:1-5**?

Perhaps Paul was remembering these words when he penned **Philippians 1:15-19**. The message is what carries the power. I experience this all the time. When I open my mouth to speak truth – God's Word – a power, confidence and boldness comes out. It never happens in my everyday life, but only when I'm speaking God's message. I do believe, however, that the message will have greater impact when the motives behind it are pure. Either way, though, Paul rejoiced that the message was going out.

Now, let's conclude with some principles from this passage of Scripture.

Don't let mean people steal your joy!

How did Paul demonstrate this principle in **verse 20?**

For those doing God's work, here's a stark reality: some will cause you grief. You *will* encounter people who will do all sorts of things out of wrong motives. It shouldn't be this way, but we live in a fallen world and the Church is made up of humans.

When this happens, follow Paul's example: shrug it off and move on! Remember that God weighs the motives of the heart and people are accountable to Him, not to you. Our witness will be stronger and will impact more people if we do everything with the purest of motives and we don't let people's mean-spirited actions defeat us. God's opinion is the most valuable one!

Focus on the ones with pure motives!

What did Paul say about these people in **verse 15**?

I remember the day I received a nasty message from a leader in the church. My heart was pulsing, and my skin was burning hot as I read each stinging word. It didn't take long for my joy to vanish in the darkness of the night. In a matter of seconds, everything good turned into ugliness. It was a horrible few hours until God brought this message before me and I started to turn my focus onto the good things and the good people in my life who encouraged me. Sometimes, though, we can stay in that place of darkness for long periods of time.

Imagine how the apostle Paul felt. In addition to the chains and the confinement, he had people – brothers in Christ – who were trying to make life more difficult for him. But instead of letting their bad behavior get him down, he practiced breathing out the ugly and breathing in the beautiful. There were *many* partnering with him in the Gospel message. This is what he focused on and what brought him such joy.

Ask for prayer!

Paul tells the Philippian believers that he was able to get through the tough times because they prayed for him **(verse 19)**.

What did the apostle Paul ask for in **2 Thessalonians 3:1-2**? Be specific.

Asking for prayer is not a sign of weakness, but a sign of strength. We see the power of prayer throughout the book of Acts – the saints praying for each other and the hand of God moving on behalf of their prayers. When we pray for our brothers and sisters, God's hand is stretched out. But they often don't know what we're going through unless we ask for prayer.

Ask for the Holy Spirit's help!

Sometimes the third person of the Trinity is overlooked – we simply forget to ask Him to help us. Let me remind you that one of the names given to the Holy Spirit is *Helper* **(John 14:26 NASB)**. His *job* is to help us. But in relation to this, we need to remember **James 4:3: "You do not have, because you do not ask."** We need to ask for the Holy Spirit's help.

As you evaluate your situation, review the principles from today's lesson, and write down the one you need to apply to your life. How will you do it?

Ponder today's *Finding Fullness of Joy* principle and write it at the back of the book.

Finding Fullness of Joy

Making God's message our focal point

1. https://www.goodreads.com/author/quotes/14919141.John_R_W_Stott
2. https://www.gotquestions.org/bondservant.html
3. https://utmost.org/classic/a-bond-slave-of-jesus-classic/
4. *Zondervan NIV Exhaustive Concordance* (Grand Rapids, MI: Zondervan Publishing Co.), 1565.
5. LOGOS, Opening up Philippians.
6. https://www.christianquotes.info/quotes-by-topic/quotes-about-unity/?listpage=2&instance=2#partici-pants-list-2
7. W. E. Vine, *Vines Complete Expository Dictionary* (Nashville, TN: Thomas Nelson, Inc.), 204.

Week 2
All for Christ

Day 1
Heavenly Perspective
Day 2
Big Dilemma
Day 3
Benefits of Progression
Day 4
Standing Against Opposers
Day 5
Christian Suffering

Evangelist Billy Sunday said, "If you have no joy, there's a leak in your Christianity somewhere." That's a bold statement, but one that is true. I don't know your circumstances or what you've been through, but I do know that the apostle Paul went through horrific things. He was beaten, shipwrecked, imprisoned, stoned, left for dead, and went for long periods of time without food and water, just to name a few things **(2 Corinthians 11:23-28)**. Yet despite all these terrible things, he was *filled* with joy.

In his letter to the Philippians, Paul does a fabulous job of showing the difference between joy and happiness. But *we* often confuse the two. So, let me untie the string that often connects joy and happiness to show how very different they are. Happiness has its source in people, events, and circumstances. It rises and falls depending on what's going on in our lives. One minute we are on top of the world gloating in glee; the next moment, we've fallen into a dark, dreary pit that seems to have no way out. You know what I'm talking about, don't you?

Joy, on the other hand, has its source in God and is a fruit of the Holy Spirit **(Galatians 5:22)**. Joy is a glorious benefit that God gives to His people – an ongoing inner serenity that is always present no matter what's going on. But here's what we need to know: while joy is a gift, it's also a *choice*, much like the attitude we choose for the day. A gift is only ours when we accept it. Joy is the same – we must embrace it to experience its fullness. And there is not a better "how to" manual to finding joy than Philippians. Hang with me this week as we uncover more principles that will surely help us on our quest for fuller joy.

Day 1
Heavenly Perspective

Joyous Jewel
For to me, to live is Christ and to die is gain. Philippians 1:21

If you grew up singing the old hymns of the church, then you remember two of my favorites: *Blessed Assurance* and *To God be the Glory*. These two hymns, filled with deep theology, were written by Fanny Crosby. Her journey to becoming a prolific hymnist, though, is quite amazing. Fanny became blind as an infant. Throughout her long life, she played several instruments – the piano, the harp, the guitar and the organ. She also wrote over 9,000 hymns. Fanny was once quoted as saying, "If I had a choice, I would still choose to remain blind...for when I die, the first face I will ever see will be the face of my blessed Savior." [1] I would say that Fanny Crosby lived with a heavenly perspective.

The way we regard situations, good or bad, is what we call *perspective*. Of course, it's easy to have a good perspective when things are going well – when everything is hunky dory. But that perspective can quickly change the moment things take a downward spiral. It's important to note that our perspective determines how we deal with heartache, brokenness, and suffering. And the outcome to those things can surely be a direct result of our perspective.

What two perspectives does Paul talk about in **Colossians 3:1-3**?

1. _____
2. _____

Which perspective does he tell us we should live with? Why?

Write out what you think a *heavenly perspective* looks like.

The apostle Paul, like Fanny Crosby, lived with a *heavenly* perspective. And there's not a better passage in all his writings that reveals this more than our passage today.

Slowly read **Philippians 1:20-21** and write down your first thoughts.

If you're wondering how you can have a perspective like Paul's, then we need to examine these verses closer. Here are three things to help us achieve a heavenly perspective...

To achieve a heavenly perspective, we need to...

Expect *God's* outcome!

Using **Philippians 1:20**, fill in the blanks:

I eagerly expect and hope that I will in no way be _____, but will have sufficient _____ so that now as always Christ will be _____ in my body, whether by life or by death.

Now, write down all three words from the three blanks:

_____

_____

_____

This verse is clear on one thing: no matter what happened, Paul would find joy in God's outcome. Rather than shake his fist in God's face and complain that his circumstances were not favorable, he believed God would use them for His glory. God would never allow shame to wash over him, He would give him courage to face whatever happened, and God would use his body as a vessel for His glory. Hence, the apostle Paul trusted that God would be exalted in his body, even if he died. He was perfectly content being **"poured out like a drink offering" (2 Timothy 4:6)**. Paul surely had a confident expectation of meeting Christ.

Centuries later, Paul's anointed writings have been included in the archives of Scripture. His letters have become some of the most valued doctrine in the church. In fact, one third of the New Testament was written by Paul. But here's what we need to remember: at the time of the writing of Philippians, Paul did not know how God would use his circumstances. Surely, he was vague on the outcome details. He did, however, believe it would all turn out for the good.

What did Joseph say to his brothers in **Genesis 50:20**?

Imagine being one of Joseph's brothers on this day? Certainly, this was not the response they ever expected. I wonder how often they remembered the younger brother they had sold to the Egyptian caravan years before. How could this abandoned brother go from slave to overseer? How was it possible that they were now standing before the brother they had once disregarded like a piece of trash and then lied about to their father? And how could Joseph offer them forgiveness? You see, God had a glorious outcome. Through His sovereign nature, God turned tragedy into triumph.

Perhaps this story was mulling around in Paul's mind when he put aside his own ideas and expected God's outcome. No doubt, he was more concerned about God's plan going forth than his own comfort. How God would use it, he did not know. But, he trusted that God's sovereign will would be done.

What are you going through right now? Are your circumstances less than favorable? Are you worried and fretting about the outcome? Look up the following Scriptures and write down what God says to you:

Isaiah 46:10-11:

Psalm 33:11:

Proverbs 19:21:

Isaiah 8:10:

How do these words change your perspective?

Exist for Christ!

If I asked you what your guiding principle in life is – the motto you live by – what would you say? Write it down.

We don't have to read any further than **Philippians 1:21** to discover what Paul's motto was. What guided him in life?

We've heard this verse, **Philippians 1:21**, more times than we can count. We don't have to be Bible scholars to know that these words were pretty much at the core of Paul's existence. Therefore, it's important we gain a little more information behind this saying. Look up the following passages and write out how Paul existed on Christ.

1 Corinthians 2:1-3:

1 Corinthians 11:1:

Philippians 3:7-9:

Philippians 3:10-11:

We exist on many things: food, water, people, work, church, ministry, material things, and seeking to live a healthy lifestyle. Sometimes those things are at the core of our existence, whether we want to admit it or not. Paul sets a powerful example for us, though. He *lived* to proclaim the Gospel of Jesus Christ, imitate Christ, and pursue the knowledge of Jesus Christ. Paul willingly gave up everything that prevented him from gaining Christ. The persecutor-turned-preacher simply existed *for* Christ. Imagine *that* homecoming. I dream of the day I see Jesus. I know that my homecoming, and yours too, will be so much grander if we choose to exist for Christ like Paul did.

Live with an eternal focus!

Again, what did the apostle Paul say? Fill in the blank from **Philippians 1:21**…

For to me, to live is Christ _____.

You know the adage, "I'm just passing through!" Well, it's true. In the first century, Christian persecution was growing. Believers could be tortured or killed in unbelievable ways. Paul knew that. Yet, he wasn't afraid to die. In fact, he couldn't wait to get to his eternal home. As Paul got older, the thoughts of heaven got sweeter.

We will continue our topic of heaven in our next lesson; but for now, why do you think Paul looked at heaven as a gain from the following Scriptures?

John 14:2:

Isaiah 25:8:

Colossians 3:4:

1 Corinthians 15:55:

When Paul's struggles zapped his energy, the persecuted saints weighed heavy on his heart, and he felt the burden of the problems in the Church; his mind traveled to another place – a place of promise. Jesus promised to take him to this place – a place where tears and disgrace would be erased, the glory of God would be manifested, and temptation to sin would be absent. Surely, death was gaining to him.

Paul gives us a beautiful reminder that we need to live with an eternal focus.

Friends, we've just learned how to live with a heavenly perspective. I hope you gained a ton of valuable insight from today's lesson. Write down what God is speaking to you about as you reflect on today's *Finding Fullness of Joy* principle. Then write it at the back of the book.

Finding Fullness of Joy

Living with a heavenly perspective in the good and the bad

Day 2
Big Dilemma

Joyous Jewel

If I am to go on living in the body, this will mean fruitful labor for me. Yet what shall I choose? I do not know. Philippians 1:22

Several years ago, we decided to move from Michigan to South Carolina. So we put our house on the market and prepared our transition to the south. But in our search for a house that would meet our needs, we couldn't find one. Hence, we decided to build. In the meantime, our house in Michigan sold. And it would be months before our house in South Carolina was done and ready for occupancy. I felt displaced. In limbo. For the first time in my life, it felt as though I didn't belong anywhere. It was a weird feeling.

For true followers of Jesus, we sort of feel the same. Paul says, **"But our citizenship is in heaven. And we eagerly await a Savior from there, the Lord Jesus Christ" (Philippians 3:20).** The reality is that earth is our temporary home. And hitting the sixty-year mark last year, I can say that life seems to go by at the speed of light. A friend older than me once said, "the older we get, the more we long for heaven." Oh, how true this is. Observing the degradation of the world, my eighty-three-year-old mom often says, "There's not enough room in this world for me." I've surely seen her longing for heaven grow as she ages.

Paul was getting older, too. At the writing of Philippians, he knew his life could end at any moment. And through his writings, one can sense his longing for heaven. Thinking about heaven must have offered him incredible hope. His dilemma was real. I pray that you and I will have the same dilemma. We should be encouraged in our study today.

Our lesson is a continuation from Day 1. Read **Philippians 1:22-24**.

Write out Paul's dilemma.

Why do you think he struggled with this?

I was talking to a Christian friend the other day and she said, "I'm excited to go to heaven, but I'm not ready to leave here yet. I still have so much more to do." Another believer friend recently told me that she kind of likes it here and she hopes to stay for a while longer. Here's my two-cents on this… If we had just a quick glimpse into heaven, I think we would have the same mindset as Paul.

Based on **2 Corinthians 12:1-4**, why do you think Paul's dilemma was so real?

We don't have any more information about Paul's "heaven" experience than what's written here, but we do know he was given a glimpse. And it was so incredible he couldn't even talk about it. If he were before us right now and we asked him about this encounter, he'd probably say, "Words cannot describe what I saw and heard." We can only imagine!

Fill in the blanks from **Philippians 1:23**:

I am torn between the two: I desire to _____ and be _____ Christ, which is _____ by far.

This verse offers us three amazing features about heaven. Let's look at them.

Heaven *is* a departure!

We don't like to think about death. It scares us. It makes us uncomfortable. But we do like thinking about pleasant things – like vacations filled with beautiful scenery, colorful landscapes, and scrumptious food. Paul's verbiage in this passage – *I desire to depart* – doesn't sound much different. I think he looked at death like we look at an upcoming trip. It was simply a departure from this place. A glorious departure! Dr. Billy Graham seemed to have the same mindset when he said, *"Someday you will read or hear that Billy Graham is dead. Don't you believe a word of it. I shall be more alive than I am now. I will just have changed my address. I will have gone into the presence of God."*

This word *depart* comes from the Greek word *analyo* and has two literal meanings: 1) to loose like an anchor, [2] and 2) to strike one's tent. [3] Paul may have had the latter meaning in mind when he envisioned the departure simply because he was a tentmaker by trade and he refers to our earthly bodies as tents.

Give a description of those tents from **2 Corinthians 5:1-4**.

Paul tells us that to **"be absent from the body is to be present with the Lord"** (**2 Corinthians 5:8 KJV**). Hence, there is *no* waiting. No lounging between two places. The moment we depart this earth, we are in heaven. Our earthly tent is gone forever.

How is the new body explained in **1 Corinthians 15:42-44?**

Heaven *is* the presence of Christ!

Describe heaven based on **Revelation 5:9-14**. Take note of where Jesus is in this passage.

I don't know one person that isn't excited about being reunited with loved ones in heaven. In addition to my dad and sister, I can't wait to see my grandma again. She lived with us when I was growing up but died when I was twenty, some forty years ago. I can still hear her speaking every name of her granddaughters before she got to the one she was addressing. I'm also excited to finally meet the grandfathers I never knew. What a reunion!

But there's one reunion that will prevail above all others – the reunion with Jesus, the One who sits on the throne. We've chased after Him. We've abided in Him. Imagine standing before Him and looking into the most beautiful eyes and feeling His tender touch on your shoulders. Imagine bowing to Him and having your eyes opened to His absolute brilliance. And if we listen hard enough, we may be able to hear sweet heavenly music playing in the background. Surely, the main attraction of heaven will be *Jesus*.

What position are believers given in heaven, according to **Romans 8:17**?

Scottish preacher William Barclay said, *"For the Christian, heaven is where Christ is. We do not need to speculate on what heaven will be like. It is enough to know that we will forever be with Him."* [4]

What do you say to that?

Heaven *is* far better!

Have you ever felt such gratitude that you said, "It doesn't get any better than this?" Well, here's what the apostle Paul would say to that… *Oh, yes it does*! I'm pretty sure this is what Paul is trying to convey when, referring to heaven, he says, **"which is better by far."** Namely, there is NOTHING you've seen, experienced, felt, encountered, touched, or sensed that is better than heaven. We may not understand it, but we *can* believe it.

Write down your most glorious picture about heaven, even if it's in your thoughts. Describe every remarkable feature.

I'm sure your illustrious picture was truly incredible, but it surely doesn't compare to the all-encompassing beauty and life in heaven.

Oh, the arrival! It's gonna be so sweet!

What are you looking forward to the most about heaven?

Now, read again our key passage **Philippians 1:22-24**.

What word would you use to describe Paul in this passage?

Your word may be different than mine and that's okay. There's not a right or wrong answer. I chose the word *surrendered*. Surrender is when we willingly give up something for the greater good. In this case, Paul gave up his own desires for God's design.

What was God's design for Paul, according to **Philippians 1:24**?

We will delve into this a bit more in our next lesson, but obviously God wasn't done with Paul yet. He still had more work for him to do, and that meant he would have to stay behind a little longer. Paul had seen heaven. He knew that life would be so much grander in paradise with Jesus – the One he had come to love and worship. The One he had served for years. But God wasn't ready to bring him home yet. So, Paul gladly accepted God's design.

How did Jesus demonstrate surrender in **Luke 22:41-43**?

Write out Jesus' words in **Luke 22:42**.

I believe Jesus told us how important surrender is when He said, **"If anyone would come after me, he must *deny* himself and take up his cross and follow me" (Matthew 16:24)**. The cross to us is a cherished symbol – one of hope, forgiveness, salvation, and love. But in Jesus' day, the cross represented death – a torturous death. Romans forced convicted criminals to carry their own cross to their death. So, taking up one's cross means being willing to die to follow Jesus. It's a dying to self. It's giving up our wants, dreams, and will for Jesus. For His design.

Surrendering demands sacrifice. We may have to sacrifice our comforts, our ideas, our plans. And it could mean sacrificing our friends, family, career, or reputation. But here's something we need to always keep in mind: while surrender is hard, the reward is worth the price. I think that's what Paul is talking about. The reward he received for surrendering his desires for God's design was well worth it in the end.

Is God asking you to surrender something? Something that is possibly standing in your way from following Him whole-heartedly? Write out your prayer.

Take a moment to ponder the *Finding Fullness of Joy* principle and write it down at the back of your book.

Finding Fullness of Joy

Surrendering our desires for His design

Day 3
Benefits of Progression

Joyous Jewel
Convinced of this, I know that I will remain, and I will continue with all of you for your progress and joy. Philippians 1:25

If you are a believer, then your purpose is to bring awareness to Jesus Christ. Your journey and my journey are certainly different, yet each of us is to be the salt and light in this world **(Matthew 5:13-16)**. Life is often hard. Circumstances can be overwhelming. Dreams will be shattered. But each of us has a purpose. God says so.

A Christian Facebook friend just posted about her loneliness, anxiety, and stress. Over the years, she's documented her many difficulties, including estrangement from her kids and childhood abuse. I've prayed for her many times. Just today she said, "I can't do this anymore." She then talked about heaven and her hope that God calls her home soon. I wonder if she wants to give up, rather than to carry on.

I know my friend is not alone in her struggle. You might be able to relate. Maybe you've felt the exact same way – life has become too big of a burden. The weight on your shoulders is getting heavier by the day. The clouds are getting darker. Well, I believe today's lesson will be an encouragement to each one of us – an encouragement to keep on keeping on.

Read **Philippians 1:24-26**.

We concluded our previous lesson with **verse 24** and we begin today with this verse. These words serve as a bridge in Paul's thought process.

Write out **Philippians 1:24**.

Review our previous lesson. Again, what was Paul's dilemma?

What is Paul's resolution? Why?

Relate **Matthew 9:35-36** to Paul's dilemma.

If sheep are without a shepherd, they will wander away, get lost, and become easy targets for the enemy. Sheep cannot survive without a shepherd. A flock needs to have a capable, caring and nurturing shepherd – a shepherd who will take care of them and cultivate their growth. Leaders in the Bible are often called shepherds (**1 Peter 5:2**). God puts them in charge of flocks. Every flock needs a qualified and loving leader. Good teachers and leaders are *vital* to the prosperity of the church. Considering this, Paul recognized that the Philippian church still needed a loving shepherd.

The apostle Paul gave a fabulous farewell address to the elders of the Ephesian church. I believe his words show the mark of an exemplary leader. Read **Acts 20:17-38** and write down words that describe his leadership.

Imagine the strength these elders left with that day. Oh, the joy that must have been evident on their faces because of this powerful encounter with their fearless leader. Here's my short list of some qualities evident in Paul from this story:

Humble (v. 19)	**Servant (v. 19)**
Committed (v. 20)	**Impartial (v. 21)**
Spirit-led (v. 22)	**Fearless (v. 22)**
Spirit-filled (v. 23)	**Faithful (v. 24)**
Shepherd (v. 28)	**Prophet (v. 31)**
Not greedy (v. 33)	**Pray-er (v. 36)**

Now, go back to **verse 27**. What other quality makes a *great* Christian leader?

I think we often overlook this one in the Church. We've become adept at preaching what's comfortable, what people want to hear. Heaven forbid we offend someone. Well, let me tell you… Paul didn't hold anything back. He proclaimed the WHOLE Word of God. Oh, how we need this more in the 21st century church. Rarely do we hear sermons on the consequences of sin, sexual purity, the value of life, and God's design for marriage. Here's the undeniable truth: these things *are* in the Bible. God has set up His blueprint for daily living and we need to teach it. Jesus didn't hold back. Paul didn't hold back. Church leaders shouldn't either.

This past Sunday my husband and I were visiting an out-of-town church. The pastor was beginning a new message series on love and relationships based on Song of Solomon (a.k.a. Song of Songs). He stood before a large congregation and powerfully expounded on the sanctity of marriage and that God designed sex for inside marriage, not outside of it. After the service, my husband and I agreed that while his message was spot on, he did not back up his claims with Scripture. While we knew this to be the truth, others may have thought, "Well, you've said it, but where does it say this in the Bible?" We should *always* back up our claims with Scripture.

On a side note: what does the Bible say about the sanctity of marriage in **Hebrews 13:4**?

I hope you've realized that Christian leadership encompasses many different facets. Review the leadership features and write out which ones you have succeeded at and which ones you may need to work on. What's your plan for the ones you need to work on?

Look back at our key passage, **Philippians 1:24-26**. What does Paul reveal about his reasons for staying behind as their leader?

I remember a teacher in High School that loved to fail his students. Oftentimes his class was the only thing that kept a student from graduating. I often wonder why teachers like this choose such a profession. But the reality is that in every school, there are good teachers and not-so-good teachers. Occasionally though, a student finds an *exemplary* teacher. This kind of teacher hates the idea of just one student failing. Hence, this teacher provides extra help and guidance to struggling students. Sometimes he or she will tutor them on their own time, give them extracurricular activities to boost their grade, or offer them helpful resources. This teacher will do whatever they can to help students succeed.

An excellent Christian leader is one who longs to see his followers progress in their faith. Witnessing deep maturity brings great joy to a leader's heart. He's worked hard, has given his time and energy to train his followers, sacrificed a lot to lead the ones God has entrusted to him, and mentored those with weaker faith. No doubt, Paul has invested into the lives of the Philippian believers. And he's filled with joy watching their progress abound.

What two things is Paul joyful about in **Philippians 1:25**?

Paul was so joyful at the thought of their progress and joy in the faith that he would willingly postpone his homegoing to help them gain a little more – to advance further. Maturity in Christ is something we should all strive for. God never intended for us to be stagnant Christians – bumps on the log, so to speak.

What is the exhortation in **1 Timothy 4:7-8**?

According to these verses, why should we train ourselves to be godly?

We live in a world that is always progressing forward – always striving to make things better. In just my lifetime, I've witnessed the computer age come alive, the Internet explode onto the scene, and cell phones become a household amenity. We've seen tremendous advancement in technology, medicine and medical research, and communication. We read in the book of Daniel that in the end days, **"Many will go here and there to increase knowledge" (Daniel 12:4)**. Thus, we will see an increase in travel and knowledge. I'm sure you realize that this prophesy is being fulfilled before our eyes.

Progression in the world has served to advance the gospel in so many ways. God has given me an online community of Bible study students. Social media has been a tool to spread truth across the world. World advancement is good, but advancement of our faith reaps earthly benefits *and* heavenly rewards.

The apostle Paul speaks to Timothy about progressing his faith. What is his admonition in **1 Timothy 4:12-15**?

For those of us that are visual learners, it's helpful to see it written out. So I've listed the things that will contribute to progression of our faith from Paul's letter to Timothy. Next to each one, write out how you can advance in each area:

Speech:

Life:

Love:

Faith:

Purity:

Scripture:

Exercising spiritual gift:

What is God speaking to you about right now? Write down your thoughts.

Take a moment to ponder the *Finding Fullness of Joy* principle and then write it down at the back of your book.

Finding Fullness of Joy
Allowing others the opportunity to invest in our lives

Day 4
Standing Against Opposers

Joyous Jewel

Whatever happens, conduct yourselves in a manner worthy of the gospel of Christ. Philippians 1:27

For over a decade, a Texas school district used a local church's sanctuary to host their graduation ceremonies. But it all ended abruptly when a group of atheists, agnostics, and free-thinkers asked the church to remove a large cross on top of the roof of the building. The leaders of the church refused, and since the school board didn't fight it, the church will no longer be hosting public school activities. Friends, these kinds of things are escalating in our country. Christians are coming against opposing forces every day.

The apostle Paul also knew opposition well. In every city, he was met with warm greetings from fellow believers, but also many people who opposed him. They hated his message, his love for Jesus, and his popularity. These enemies often joined forces together and caused great havoc for Paul. And from his letter, it seemed that the Philippian believers also confronted much opposition. So, he takes a little space in his writing to address this subject and to offer valuable advice to help them stand against opposers.

Read **Philippians 1:27-28** and write down the theme of these verses.

Our lesson today is relevant to today's believer simply because we will continue to be opposed by angry adversaries. But Paul tells us exactly how to stand up when they are trying to bring us down. Based on our passage, here are four effective ways…

Stand worthy! *"Conduct yourselves in a <u>manner worthy</u> of the gospel of Christ."*

Write down Paul's admonition in **Philippians 1:27**.

The word *worthy* comes from the Greek word *axios* and means, "to reflect God's character and thoughts." [5] So while our membership in God's family comes with huge perks, it also comes with great responsibility. It's our duty to represent God's kingdom well.

How are we to live, according to **Ephesians 4:1**?

What does this mean to you?

Why are we urged to stand worthy **(2 Thessalonians 2:12)**?

If a pastor of a church lied to his congregation, stole from the collection plate, lived by different standards than what he preached, or treated his staff with contempt; he would not be a good representative of the church or of the kingdom of God. That is *not* how Jesus operated and those kinds of things bring disrepute to the cause of Christ.

When we represent something, we stand in place of it or symbolize it. Subsequently, we show people the best side of what we're representing by adhering to its values and virtues. As Christians and members of the body of Christ, we are representatives of the kingdom of God. We are Christ's ambassadors. His messengers. It's a privilege to be called a Christian. And it's an honor to represent the One who died for us and offered us abundant and eternal life.

In what ways can we represent Jesus Christ?

Why do you think that being good representatives of the kingdom of God helps us to stand against opposers?

Stand firm! *"I know that you will stand firm."*

One definition to the word *firm* means, "not soft or yielding when pressed; securely fixed in place."

What is the exhortation in the following Scriptures?

Ephesians 6:11:

1 Peter 5:9:

Philippians 4:1:

The Christian walk is challenging. We can crack easy. We have an enemy roaming this earth looking for someone – anyone – to devour **(1 Peter 5:8)**. He's strong and uses people to come against us – opposers. Thereupon, the authors of the New Testament urge us to stand firm because Satan can pick out a weak and vulnerable soul a thousand miles away. Like blood lures a hungry shark, a little crack attracts the devil.

Unfortunately, the Church has become weaker, not stronger. Rather than standing firm, they've been lured away by the pleasures of this world and watered-down messages. The substance that was once at the core of the Church is barely recognizable anymore. Believers have so many cracks – cracks that can be easily pried open by the enemy.

How can we stand firm, according to **2 Thessalonians 2:15**?

Fellow sojourners, we can stand firm by holding onto truth. Clinging to the teachings in Scripture is the putty that seals up those cracks and creates a stronger foundation – a foundation that won't crumble even if the earth shakes. So let's putty up those cracks, plant our feet securely on the ground, and stand firm. Let's not budge – not one little bit.

Why do you think that standing firm helps us to stand against opposers?

Stand together! *"I know that you will stand firm <u>in one spirit</u>, <u>contending as one man</u> for the faith of the gospel."*

What does it say in Ecclesiastes **4:9-12**?

How should the body of Christ operate, according to **Ephesians 4:16**?

The body of Christ is comprised of people. And there is certainly power in numbers. But only when people *stand together*. Division will make any institution, corporation, family, or relationship fall. It will weaken its foundation. Standing side-by-side with others has advantages. God intended for us to work together, not stand alone.

Think of a good leadership team. What do you think keeps them together?

As I ponder standing together, a saying keeps popping into my mind:

Surround yourself with those on the same mission as you.

When I was growing up, my parents were actively involved in the church we were attending. I don't remember much about those days because I was little, but I heard my mom and dad talk about the problems for many years. The pastor and the leadership of the church did not share the same goals or vision. This brought the elders, deacons, and the pastor into sharp disagreement over many issues until the church eventually split right down the middle. Many families left, including mine. This is still a sad reality in the church today.

But here's a positive scenario...

When Billy Graham was starting out in ministry, he gathered several qualified and trustworthy comrades to join his team. From the onset, Billy told them that, in the past, some evangelists had run into difficulties and had gotten involved in things that brought dishonor to the cause of Christ. So to keep that from happening to his ministry, this team formed an alliance and held each other accountable to four virtues: 1) financial accountability; 2) moral integrity; 3) respect for the local church and its pastors; 4) truth in publicity. And these four virtues are still at the core of the Billy Graham Evangelistic Association, decades later.

This organization is still standing strong because the leadership team stood together and didn't waver. The foundation got stronger rather than weaker.

Are you standing apart from others rather than standing together with them? If so, how will you rectify this?

Why do you think that standing together helps us to stand against opposers?

Stand courageously! *"...<u>without being frightened</u> in any way by those who oppose you."*

Write out **2 Timothy 1:7**.

What did the early believers pray for when confronted with opposition **(Acts 4:29)**?

Imagine how different the world would be if believers everywhere shared the Gospel rather than shrink away from it. I do know, however, that fear keeps many from living out the Great Commission **(Matthew 28:18-20)**. But we're reminded that God gave us a spirit of power. It's ours for the asking. Something tells me that the early believers were timid at times as well. So, they prayed for *great boldness*.

Do you want courage like the early believers? Write out your prayer.

Why do you think that standing courageously helps us to stand against opposers?

Ponder the *Finding Fullness of Joy* principle and then write it at the back of the book.

Finding Fullness of Joy

Standing securely on the gospel of Jesus Christ

Day 5
Christian Suffering

Joyous Jewel

For it has been granted to you on behalf of Christ not only to believe on him, but to suffer for him. Philippians 1:29

When Jesus was at the peak of His ministry and popularity, great crowds followed Him. They watched His every move and clung to His every word. Some wondered about this man from Nazareth. Others questioned His teachings. And still others sought after Him with a vast determination. That little country of Israel was shaken up when Jesus arrived on the scene. He healed many and drew in curious followers. And His miracles usually turned into kingdom teachings – teachings about commitment and sacrifice.

One day a great multitude had followed Jesus to the mountainside and Jesus performed one of the most famous miracles of all – He fed this hungry crowd with a little boy's lunch **(John 6:1-13)**. The next day those who had been fed found Jesus across the lake. And He used this time to teach them kingdom truths **(John 6:22-59)**. He called on them to decide – to make a commitment. Would they choose Him, or would they choose the way of their forefathers? Before they raised their hand and agreed to follow Him, though, they would learn a hard truth: it wouldn't be easy. It would require great sacrifice **(John 6:60)**. In the end, many left that day. They simply walked away **(John 6:66)**. Why? Because it was just too hard.

Just like in Jesus' day, we often want the benefits that come from being a child of God, but we don't want the commitment. That's not what we signed up for. The Bible is also clear on another issue: suffering accompanies a faithful life. Not only do Jesus and the New Testament writers tell us that Christian suffering is inevitable for one living a Christ-centered life, but we know that many – in the Bible and throughout the generations that followed – suffered greatly for Christ. So we consciously or subconsciously decide not to follow fully. We think to ourselves that since our eternity is secure, that's all that matters.

I believe today's lesson will help us to get a better grip on Christian suffering. I also believe today's topic will change the way we view Christian suffering.

Read **Philippians 1:29-30**.

What has been granted to you?

What do you think "granted" means in this context?

Suppose you were granted an invitation to a White House dinner where dignitaries from around the world would be seated next to you. Or you were granted box office seats to a Super Bowl game. Or perhaps you were granted backstage access to meet your favorite singer. No doubt, every time we're granted special privileges, we consider it an honor.

I don't, however, think we consider suffering a privilege. We certainly wouldn't be jumping up and down and biting at the bit to welcome it. But Paul is telling us that suffering for Christ is exactly that – a privilege.

What was the apostles' response to suffering in **Acts 5:41**?

Public flogging was not just excruciatingly painful, but it was also humiliating. Oh, the shame that must have washed over someone who was publicly whipped and ostracized. Yet the apostles pushed those feelings aside and realized that God had a bigger purpose in all of it. I wonder if at this moment they were remembering Jesus' words. What were they?

Matthew 5:10-12:

Matthew 10:22:

John 15:18-21:

Something tells me that the apostles were looking beyond the pain and humiliation to the future reward. Years later, Peter would write to a group of believers scattered throughout Asia Minor – believers being persecuted under Roman rule. Perhaps Jesus' words and his own experiences with past and present persecution caused Peter to address Christian suffering in his letter. Let's look…

Read **1 Peter 4:12-16** and write down what Peter says about suffering for Christ.

What kinds of persecution do you think we go through?

There are four pieces to this "persecution" puzzle from this passage:

Persecution is inevitable!

What did Peter say in **1 Peter 4:12**?

Why do you think he told them not to be surprised?

These believers had heard Jesus' words many times. They also knew what the apostles and early believers had gone through. Peter wrote his letter at the very end of his public ministry – a ministry that spanned thirty years. The pastors and lay people of the churches heard about Stephen, the first martyr. They knew that some were imprisoned, beaten, ridiculed, and killed for their faith. They also heard about the wicked emperor, Nero, who was singling out Christians and killing them. So, Peter tells them that they shouldn't be surprised.

What did Paul tell Timothy in **2 Timothy 3:12**?

We are living in perilous days – the last days, no doubt – and Paul tells Timothy that persecution during those days will prevail. But here's something to think about: it's usually the bold Christians who are persecuted. People who keep their faith to themselves and blend in with the world are not harassed because no one knows they're Christians. It's easy to get away with being a nominal Christian in our country. In other places, however, being a Christian demands *great* sacrifice. Christianity is against the law in many countries and sometimes Christians are viewed as traitors. Therefore, they can lose everything, including their lives.

Christian persecution is abounding in many countries, cities, and villages across our globe. You can learn more by checking out www.persecution.com.

Persecution demands godly responses!

What does Peter urge his readers to do when persecuted for Christ **(1 Peter 4:14, 16)**?

The world doesn't understand this response to suffering. They think people like this have gone off the deep end – they're crazy. John and Betty Stam were young missionaries in communist China with a three-month old baby when they were forced to their knees and killed in front of a mocking crowd (December 8, 1934). Their little baby girl was untouched. A letter written to the mission board they served just two days before their martyrdom talked about the peace in their hearts and the gratitude they felt. Eyewitnesses said that they walked to their deaths with smiles on their faces.

What happened to Jesus **(Matthew 26:67-68)**?

What should we do when we're falsely accused or persecuted for our faith, according to **Hebrews 12:2-3**?

As you ponder these verses, what does this response do for us?

Are you suffering for Christ right now? Perhaps you're being insulted? Mocked? Or maybe someone has come against your faith. If so, how are you responding?

Persecution warrants blessing!

What truth is written in **1 Peter 4:13**?

Why is persecution good for us **(1 Peter 4:14)**?

One of the things that helps me deal with those who come against me is thinking about eternity. Someday all of this will be behind me and I'll be with Jesus. I will be **"overjoyed when his glory is revealed" (1 Peter 4:13)**. I remember an illustration that Francis Chan once gave. He held a long rope in his hands. The end of it had been colored red, which represented our earthly existence. He said that in light of eternity, the red is just a speck. But the rest is never-ending. That illustration struck me, and I often think of it when others mock my faith.

Persecution is a sign that the Spirit of God rests on us!

Write out **1 Peter 4:14**.

This last point is so important. If you are truly living your life for Christ and standing on the side of truth, people will come against you. Even people in the church. But here's the best part... this is a sure sign that the Spirit of God is on you and is actively working in you. This makes me smile. There's nothing that I want more than to be alive in the Spirit.

Based on this, write out your prayer to God.

Returning to **Philippians 1:29-30**, what is God speaking to you about right now? Write your answer and then reflect upon the *Finding Fullness of Joy* principle and write it down at the back of the book.

Finding Fullness of Joy
learning to rejoice in suffering

1. http://www.azquotes.com/author/26216-Fanny_Crosby
2. LOGOS: Commentary Critical and Explanatory on the Whole Bible.
3. LOGOS: Wuest's Word Studies in the Greek New Testament.
4. https://www.christianquotes.info/top-quotes/14-inspiring-quotes-about-heaven/#axzz56Rt6kF95
5. W. E. Vine, *Vines Complete Expository Dictionary* (Nashville, TN: Thomas Nelson, Inc.), 687.

Week 3
To Please God

Day 1
Successful Relationships
Day 2
Selfless Living
Day 3
Adopting Christ's Attitude
Day 4
Exaltation of Christ
Day 5
Working Out Your Salvation

The Roman army was a powerful force to be reckoned with. With their strong discipline and extensive organization skills, they were successful in battle. Victorious! Roman troops always fought in formation, *as a group*, and this made them quite powerful especially against less organized enemies who frequently fought with little formation. They would often link their shields together to make a line of defense. It reminds me of the great motto, *United we stand, divided we fall*.

Something tells me that you and I want success in our lives, in our relationships, in our ministries, and in our marriages. In fact, God wants us to be successful more than we do. He wants to see us thrive. Here's something to remember: even if we've faltered in some area, or fallen repeatedly, we can still go on to claim victory. We *can* achieve success.

This week we examine one of the most quoted portions of this letter, **Philippians 2:1-13**. I wonder if the apostle Paul had the Roman army in mind when he wrote that unity is essential for the success of the Church. He encourages togetherness, humbleness, and copying the same attitude that Jesus had. There is no doubt that this passage of Scripture is indispensable to the growth, stability, and survival of the Church. In fact, the principles we will study are necessary for prosperity in all aspects of life. Join me this week as we explore Paul's letter further.

Day 1
Successful Relationships

Joyous Jewel

Make my joy complete by being like-minded, having the same love, being one in Spirit and purpose. Philippians 2:2

We've noticed that the apostle Paul is focusing on fullness of joy in his letter to the Philippian church. In my opinion, there's not anything better than having a joyful spirit and being around others who are also joyful. As Paul tries to convey joy, he also notices that some in this congregation are robbing others of it. And he hits the nail on the head when he details exactly what will steal our joy. We probably aren't surprised to find that *people* can be the biggest stealer of joy. People are often the greatest challenges we face. But people are also a huge part of our lives.

According to **Romans 12:2**, how are Christians supposed to behave?

When we accepted Jesus as our Lord and Savior, He put His Spirit in us. We belong to Him. And Christians should not act or behave like the world. But the reality is that it's often hard to pick out the Christians from the non-believing world. Why is that? Well, it's because we have a sinful nature. And Paul tells us that our fleshly nature and our spiritual nature are "in conflict" with one another **(Galatians 5:17)**. Hence, they are at war. Therefore, this is a struggle believers face every day. Giving into our fleshly nature is usually easier than surrendering to our spiritual nature.

How do you see this in your own life? In the life of believers around you?

People can be hurtful, prideful, spiteful, careless, heartless, thoughtless, and tactless. I'm pretty sure you've been the victim of all of these "sinful nature" problems, *and* you've also been on the other end and acted as the culprit in letting these things reign. No doubt, Paul recognized this problem in the church at Philippi, so he addressed it.

What is Paul's message in **Philippians 2:1-2**?

Before we dig into this message, keep in mind that the Church is not full of perfect people, but it *is* full of people who have been redeemed. Yes, Jesus paid the full price for our sin. He delivered us from the penalty of death and gave us life. When people do something nice for us, we usually repay them by doing something nice in return. This is how we should respond to Jesus – we should repay Him for what He did for us by living the way He instructed us to live.

The Church is always being threatened. Often the threat comes from the outside, but the biggest threat is usually from within. And one huge offender is *discord*. Nothing divides and destroys faster than when people don't get along. And sometimes we just need incentives to get us moving in the right direction. Obviously, the Philippian church did too.

Paul outlines four influencing motives in **Philippians 2:1** to spur them toward unity. In your own words, write out what each one means to you:

Encouragement from being united with Christ:

Comfort from His love:

Fellowship with the Spirit:

Tenderness and compassion:

One year during Vacation Bible School when I was young, my church offered a fabulous prize for memorizing the most Bible verses: a puppy. Because I love dogs so much, you better believe I went to town memorizing. The hard work paid off in the end and I won the cutest little beagle. Oh, how proud I was to bring that little guy home. Sometimes we need a catalyst to incite us to act. Successful and profitable businesses are masters at offering incentives to their employees; whether it's a year-end bonus, a free vacation, or a practical gift. Good incentives always work to spur people on.

The apostle Paul uses the same tactic to push the people toward unity. He doesn't offer a gift or a bonus, but rather he appeals to their emotional side by reminding them of what Jesus did for them. For believers, nothing should motivate us more.

How do the above incentives motivate you in your Christian journey?

Review the incentives and write a thank-you note to Jesus.

Paul's main goal in this section is to see the people come together in unity. Let me remind you that every relationship, every church, and every institution is comprised of imperfect humans. Dissension and differences are par for the course. We come from different walks of life and most of us have strong opinions. And some people are stubborn, not easily bendable. The Philippian church surely had a variety of people in their midst: Jewish converts, Gentile businessmen, and Roman leaders. Some were wealthy and others poor. But unity must be at the core for the church to succeed and bring glory to the cause of Christ. So in **Philippians 2:2**, Paul offers three pieces to the unity puzzle.

Being like-minded:

What does being like-minded mean to you?

This word *like-minded* literally means "to think the same thing." [1]

How are we to live, according to **Romans 12:16**?

In music, two or more sounds come together to make one beautiful harmony. The word *harmony* is the same word as like-minded. This is a perfect example of what it is to live in harmony with others – there should always be a common place to meet. The Bible doesn't tell us to throw away our ideas, but to find a meeting ground of compromise. We may need to bend a little more or surrender our fleshly desires. Being like-minded is certainly the first step to unity.

Based on **2 Corinthians 13:11**, what is the result of living in peace with others?

Is there someone you are at odds with? If so, what will you do to remedy the situation?

Having the same love:

Write out **1 Peter 4:8**.

What does this verse mean to you? How do you see this truth at work?

Think of love as a bridge. A bridge that brings people together. People respond to love. If we love more, we have less selfishness, less arguing, less discord, less division, less bitterness, less pride, and less anger. Love surely covers a *multitude* of sins.

Love unites! Hate divides!

Give a description of love based on **1 Corinthians 13:1-12**.

What are two important things you learn about love from **1 Corinthians 13:8, 13**?

What does **Colossians 3:13-14** tells us about love and unity?

Is love a missing component in your life? What will you do to love more?

Being one in spirit and purpose:

This point is sort of a continuation of being like-minded. A church can't survive if believers don't agree on doctrine. There's an interesting story in **Acts 15**. In the early days of the church, a disagreement arose in Antioch. Some leaders from the church in Jerusalem came to Antioch and informed the Gentile believers that they needed to be circumcised to be saved. Paul and Barnabas debated with these leaders to no avail. Finally, the church in Antioch sent them to the church in Jerusalem to consult with the apostles and elders. After much discussion, they resolved the issue and the leaders were on the same page.

What does **1 Corinthians 1:10** instruct us to do?

How much effort should we put into practicing unity, according to **Ephesians 4:3**?

What should we do when we disagree with others?

Truth be told, we can only scratch the surface in our research on unity since the Bible is filled with teachings about unity. I think God wants us to take this topic seriously since He spends so much time addressing it. There's nothing that brings more honor to Christ and more success to our churches and our relationships than unity.

Ponder today's *Finding Fullness of Joy* principle and write it at the back of the book.

Finding Fullness of Joy

Working hard at getting along with people

Day 2
Selfless Living

Joyous Jewel
Do nothing out of selfish ambition or vain conceit. Philippians 2:3

There is no doubt we live in a *self*-generation. Whether people are taught it or not, they often live with themselves at the center of their universe. No wonder divorce is rampant, relationships are broken, and people are walking around in severe identity crises. Our lesson today reveals God's ways, and it is often *not* the ways most people are living. God's ways are almost always in opposition to the ways of the world. And if we choose to live according to God's pattern, we will fare so much better and have fuller joy. Today we observe the difference between selfish living and *selfless* living.

We've heard about the "selfie" generation. What does that phrase mean to you? How do you see it at work in the world?

Here are a few quotes to ponder:

If you live your life as if everything is about you, you will be left with just that. Just you.

The emptiest people on this planet are usually the ones fullest of themselves.

A self-absorbed person can only see the faults of others. They are often color blind to their own.

Do you agree with these sayings? Explain.

Here's the thing: we need to stop embracing the lies of the enemy and start listening to what God has to say. Today's lesson is relevant for every aspect of our lives. If we learn to live selfless rather than selfish, then we'll dwell in greater peace and have better relationships.

What is the basic theme of **Philippians 2:3-4**?

In these verses, Paul does a superb job of detailing how to achieve selfless living. He offers two *don'ts* and two *dos*. If we can learn to master these things, we'll see success all over the board. Let's begin with the don'ts…

Don't be selfish!

Fill in the blanks from **Philippians 2:3**: Do _____ out of _____ _____…

The Greek word for selfish ambition is *eritheia*, and the ancient Greek philosopher Aristotle defined selfishly ambitious people as "those who want to achieve political office by making themselves look bigger and better before others through trickery." [3] The Bible compares someone using trickery or deception to an antichrist: **"Many deceivers, who do not acknowledge Jesus Christ as coming in the flesh, have gone out into the world. Any such person is the deceiver and the antichrist" (2 John 1:7).**

Where does selfish ambition originate **(Galatians 5:19)**?

Selfish ambition is at the heart of our fallen nature and will surely ruin *any* relationship. Nothing good ever comes from selfish ambition.

What do you learn about selfish ambition from **James 3:14-16**?

These are such strong words and a powerful warning to each of us. The world applauds selfish ambition, God does not. We surely need to evaluate our motives from time to time and make sure that selfish ambition is not driving our actions.

Now would be a good time to evaluate our motives. Are you experiencing a failed relationship? A faltering partnership? A dysfunctional team? A division in some area of your life? Write down what God is speaking to you about.

Don't be prideful!

Fill in the blanks from **Philippians 2:3: Do nothing out of selfish ambition or** _____ _____…

The Greek word for *vain conceit* (or *vainglory* in the KJV) is *kenodoxia* and means, "a state of pride that has no proper basis." [4] It's used to describe a person who has a puffed-up idea of one's own importance.

How does God look at pride in **1 Peter 5:5**?

Based on this verse, it would be accurate to say that if pride is driving our actions, then God is against us. That's strong language, don't you agree? Perhaps God wants us to understand how serious the sin of pride is. You've heard it said that **"pride goes before destruction, a haughty spirit before a fall" (Proverbs 16:18)**.

Why do you think God opposes the proud?

Allow me to chime in on this a little. The heart of pride is focused on self. Therefore, prideful people become jealous of others' success. Two key components to pride are independence and rebellion. The sinful nature leads us to desire independence and we rebel at the thought of being under anyone's control or authority, even God's. When all our focus is on self, the result leads to self-pity, anger, bitterness, envy, jealousy, and a hard heart toward God.

Why is pride so detrimental, based on **Psalm 10:4**?

Do you understand why pride is at the root of most of our relationship issues and the cause of many divisions in the church? What is God saying to you right now?

I love that God doesn't leave us in the dark. He always gives us a remedy to fix the broken stuff. Our lesson today ends on a positive note and gives us two "dos" that can surely keep us unified with others and help to solidify our relationships. Let's look...

Do be humble!

Fill in the blank from **Philippians 2:3**: ...but in _____ consider others better than yourselves.

This word *humility* means, "lowliness of mind." One pastor described it as "having no thoughts about yourself." Biblical humility is the opposite of pride and is a godly character trait that will show forth in someone who truly follows Jesus. We often confuse biblical humility with worldly humility. Worldly humility believes that being humble means you are not worth anything and you are sort of like a floor mat – you let people walk all over you. This is *not* biblical humility.

Explain your value based on **1 Peter 2:9-10**.

Describe the way God sees you **(Deuteronomy 7:6)**.

How much precision did God put forth to create you, according to **Psalm 139:13-16**?

59

So if God calls you holy and treasured, and He went to great detail to knit you together in your mother's womb, then He must think you're pretty special and worthy. Therefore, you shouldn't think of yourself as anything less. Humility is *not* thinking of ourselves as insignificant or unimportant, but it's seeing ourselves as lower than God and voluntarily submitting to His will. A Christ-centered humility creates unity and softens our hearts.

What will you do to become more humble in your actions?

Do be respectful!

According to **Philippians 2:4**, how can we show respect for others?

What does this mean to you?

Many people are beating themselves up while living in guilt. They have poor self-images. Sometimes it can be traced back to their childhood, the rejection they endured in life, or weights they have placed on their own shoulders. In any case, you and I can help them overcome such bondage by putting their needs above our own.

Based on **Romans 12:10**, what does showing respect do for people?

The world tells us to look out only for ourselves. We are more important than anything else. The Bible differs on this. Jesus put our needs above His own when He left heaven to come here. We will discuss this in greater detail in our next lesson, but if Jesus did that for us, we can certainly do this for others. Respecting others by putting their needs above our own is one sure tool that can fix broken relationships and bring unity.

Is there someone you need to show respect to? How will you do it?

God is moving in my spirit today. I hope He's doing the same thing to you. Oh, how important today's topic is. Write out what God is saying to you as you ponder today's *Finding Fullness of Joy* principle. Then write it at the back of the book.

Finding Fullness of Joy

Putting aside selfish ambition and pride for humility and respect

Day 3
Adopting Christ's Attitude

Joyous Jewel
Your attitude should be the same as that of Christ Jesus. Philippians 2:5

We come to a passage of Scripture today that you and I cannot really understand, but it's something we accept by faith. I pray that our eyes will be opened as we study one of the richest sections in all the Bible. The apostle Paul does a phenomenal job of presenting the incarnation of Jesus – when Jesus left heaven and came to earth, took on the form of a human body, and humbled Himself. Something tells me that our hearts will be captivated by this fundamental theology of the Christian faith.

Read **Philippians 2:5-8**. What do you learn about Jesus' identity from this section of Scripture?

We'll first take this passage apart and then we'll go back and look at what we are to do with this information. There's so much valuable stuff here, so we'll try to capture the essence. In relation to Jesus Christ's incarnation, there are four features to understand:

His deity (verse 6)!

What did Jesus say in **Matthew 7:13-14**?

Let me tell you that what Jesus said is true, especially when you hear what others believe about Jesus. Some have conducted surveys asking random people what they believe about Jesus. Here are a few responses:

Jesus was a pretty cool guy with a peaceful philosophy
He was good at what He did
He was a dude who lived back in the day
Jesus is a made-up story that got blown out of proportion

And here are what a few of the world's religions teach about Jesus:

Jehovah Witnesses: Jesus is not God. Before he lived on earth, he was Michael, the archangel.
Mormonism: Jesus is a separate god from the Father (Elohim). His body was created through sexual union between Elohim and Mary.

New Age: Jesus is not the one true God. He is not a savior, but a spiritual model, and guru. He was a new ager who tapped into divine power in the same way that anyone can.

Islam: Jesus is one of the most respected of over 124,000 prophets sent by Allah. Jesus was sinless, born of a virgin, and a great miracle worker, but not the Son of God.

Islam is the second largest religion, not far behind Christianity. Considering the statistics and what people say about Jesus, one can surely understand Jesus' statement that the road to destruction is wide. Any religion that does not believe in Jesus' divinity is a false religion. Paul gives us documented facts of His deity in our passage, **Philippians 2:5-8**.

The word *nature* in **verse 6** (translated *form* in the New King James Version Bible) comes from the Greek word *morphe* and means, "the character, the whole essence of deity." [5] Hence, Jesus Christ possessed the unchangeable, essential nature and character of God. It's important to note that this is referring to the inside, not just the outside. And here's another interesting fact about this phrase in **Philippians 2:6**: the word "being" is in the present active participle which means that Jesus *always* was God.

How does **John 1:1** substantiate this?

What does the second half of **Philippians 2:6** say? What does this mean to you?

Here's the awesome thing: Jesus loved us so much that He willingly put aside His equality with God to come to earth. So when He came to earth, He went under God's authority. Thus, Jesus sacrificed everything for you and me. How does this make you feel?

How does Jesus' deity form your views?

His humility (verse 7)!

How did Jesus humble Himself based on **verse 7?**

Paul tells us that [Jesus] **"made himself nothing" (verse 7)**. The New King James Version translates this as, **"He made himself of no reputation."** This is what is commonly called the "kenosis" (or the emptying). So, what did Jesus empty Himself of? First, He did *not* empty Himself of His divinity (He was still 100% God), but He did empty Himself of the prerogatives of His divinity. He set aside the right to his ultimate glory, power, and authority.

Compare **Mark 10:45** with Jesus the servant.

How do you see Jesus as the ultimate servant?

His humanity (verse 8)!

Fill in the blank based on **verse 8**: **"And being found in** _____
as a man."

Jesus traded in His heavenly body for an earthly body. He lived with physical limitations, but self-limitations as He *chose* humanity. Have you ever experienced culture shock when you visited another place or another country? I spent a summer in Guatemala during college and I must say it took a while to get adjusted to a vastly different culture, where the people lived so differently than the way I was used to living. Imagine the culture shock Jesus experienced when He left the glories of heaven to come to this place. It was surely the *ultimate* culture shock. Yet, He voluntarily did it.

How does John confirm His humanity in **John 1:14?**

Continue with this thought by looking up **1 John 1:1-3.**

What does Jesus' humanity mean for us, according to **2 Corinthians 8:9?**

Why did Jesus become poor based on the previous verse?

This is the best demonstration of love I can think of. The band Downhere sings about this in their song, *How Many Kings*: "How many kings have stepped down from their thrones? How many lords have abandoned their homes? How many greats have become the least for me? And how many gods have poured out their hearts to romance a world that is torn all apart? How many fathers gave up their sons for me?"

My heart is churning with gratitude right now. Tears are welling up in my eyes just thinking of what Jesus gave up for me. Such a huge sacrifice. Are you thankful? If so, take a few moments to ponder it and then write out what you want to say to Jesus.

His intention (verse 8)!

What was Jesus' intention – His purpose – in all of this, based on **Philippians 2:8**?

How does the writer of Hebrews explain it in **Hebrews 2:14**?

I say all the time that since Jesus came to this world and died a wretched death for my freedom, why wouldn't I give Him my life? Why wouldn't I surrender it all for Him? I am so grateful for the freedom I enjoy, the light I walk in, the hope I have every moment of every day, the Spirit of God residing inside me, and the body of Christ I belong to. With so many awesome benefits, why wouldn't I lay down my life for Him? He came here with one intention – to set us free from sin and death. And the way He did it was to die a horrible, painful, and humiliating death – a death reserved for sinners.

How does **Hebrews 12:2** describe Jesus' intention? And what was His attitude?

We could spend much more time on this section of Scripture, but time won't allow us to do that. So let's conclude our lesson with our response. What are we to do with this information, according to **Philippians 2:5**?

Review each point and then write out how your attitude should mirror Jesus' attitude.

Why do you think imitating Jesus' attitude is the best way to live?

I've heard it said that *outlook determines outcome*. I believe Paul is trying to convey in this passage of Scripture that *attitude* determines outcome. The attitude we choose can be the difference between discouragement or joy, contentment or worry. If we choose to empty ourselves of our wants and desires and put others above ourselves, then we will have less jealousy and more compassion. We will have stronger relationships, more power in ministry, and much more peace in life. God surely honors a heart that imitates His attitude.

Do you need an attitude adjustment? What is God speaking to you about? Write down your thoughts and prayer.

Ponder today's *Finding Fullness of Joy* principle and write it at the back of the book.

Finding Fullness of Joy
Changing our attitude to imitate Christ's attitude

Exaltation of Christ

Joyous Jewel
Therefore God exalted him to the highest place and gave him the name that is above every name. Philippians 2:9

You may have seen the popular bumper sticker that says "Coexist." Without giving much thought to it, one could think that this sign – a sign that speaks of living in peace with others –has a good message. But if you research it, you'll find that it's a complete contradiction to the Word of God. Each of the letters have been *substituted* with symbols – symbols representing different religions and lifestyles the world is trying to promote. Look at the picture and then read what each symbol represents...

C – the star and the crescent moon represents Islam
O – the peace sign represents the pagan Wiccan pentacle
E – the male/female sign represents gay rights or gender equality
X – the star of David represents Judaism
I – the "i" is a symbol representing paganism or witchcraft
S – the "s" is the Chinese yin-yang symbol
T – the cross represents Christianity

The main idea behind this bumper sticker is that no religion or movement is above another. And despite having different belief systems, we should all strive to coexist with one another. Hence, we should live side-by-side with others and accept whatever beliefs they have.

Our lesson today will reveal a truth at the foundation of Christianity and will show us why we should never embrace this "coexistence" foolish belief system.

Write out **Acts 4:12**:

In one sentence summarize this verse.

What was Christianity called in the early days of the church (**Acts 9:2**)?

One of the things that seemed to get Christians in trouble in the early days of the church is what they preached: that Jesus is the ONLY way. Friends, this message is still getting believers in trouble. In our world today, Christians are labeled intolerant, narrow-minded, biased, and hateful. Why? Because they firmly stand on Jesus' words: **"I am the way, and the truth, and the life. No one comes to the Father except through me" (John 14:6)**. Christians not only speak it, but they truly believe it. And today's lesson will uncover this weighty truth and hopefully, it will shake us to the core and awaken the hearts of any doubters.

Let's begin by observing **Acts 1:1-11**. What happened after Jesus rose from the dead?

Jesus never did anything without witnesses looking on. He did not want there to be any doubts, especially regarding His ascension to heaven. On this day, there were many gathered, and they saw with their very own eyes Jesus being lifted from the earth. Centuries later, we have their testimonies *and* documented proof. What they saw, they wrote down. We now turn our attention from the humility of Jesus to the exultation of Jesus.

Ponder **Philippians 2:9-11** and answer the following questions:

Who is Jesus, according to this passage?

What is His position?

What has been given to Him?

Our passage today comes on the coattails of the "emptying" passage, **Philippians 2:5-8**. Jesus came to the earth as the Son of Man but was raised as the Son of God. How was Jesus raised? Let's look at three ways…

God raised Jesus in…

Position!

What place did God give Jesus **(Philippians 2:9)**?

Where is Jesus seated right now, according to **Romans 8:34**?

In the Bible, a high-ranking person would put someone on his right hand to give him equal honor with himself and to recognize him as possessing equal dignity and authority. It's written that **"God placed all things under [Jesus'] feet and appointed him to be head over everything for** the church" **(Ephesians 1:22)**. Hence, God put Jesus on equal par with Himself. Judges command rule from the courtroom, presidents command rule from their desks, and executives command rule from their offices. Each of these are respected positions. But Jesus commands rule from heaven. There is NO higher position. He surely demands our respect.

Will you respect Jesus' position? How?

God raised Jesus in…

Title!

What do you learn about Jesus' name from **Philippians 2:9**?

Today, we often don't think of the meaning of a name before naming our babies. Some people do, but most do not. We named our children Betsy and Matthew because we liked the names. Betsy has my middle name and Matt has Lou's middle name. It wasn't until after they were born that I realized I loved the meaning of their names. In the Bible, a name identified someone.

What was Joseph told to name his son and why **(Matthew 1:20-21)**?

The Greek translation of *Jesus* means, "The Lord saves." And Jesus did exactly that – He came to save us from our sins. Jesus' name is powerful.

What do you learn about Jesus' name from the following verses?

Acts 16:18:

John 14:14:

Matthew 28:19:

Romans 10:13:

1 Corinthians 6:11:

Now, what are we to do with the name of Jesus, according to **Colossians 3:17**?

We've only skimmed the surface on the name of Jesus. But here's the thing: since the name of Jesus is higher than all other names, we should hold it in absolute sanctity. It's holy and demands our total allegiance. His name is the only one worth worshiping. When I hear Jesus' name taken in vain, I'm offended. Misusing His name *should* offend us since we have His name seared into our hearts and souls. There are many things we elevate to a worshipful position, but everything else should pale in comparison to Jesus' name.

What will you do with Jesus' name today?

God raised Jesus in…

Power and Authority!

What is the sphere of Jesus' influence and authority **(Philippians 2:10)**?

In relation to **Philippians 2:10-11**, how will God truly exalt Jesus?

Obviously, this is speaking of a future time since many do not bow to the name of Jesus. The word *confess* means to "publicly declare, to agree with someone." So one day, everyone – whether they were for Jesus or against Him – will bow before Him and publicly declare what God testified about His Son. Whether they led many astray through atheism, false religion, science, or their own selfish ambitions; they will not just stand before Jesus, but they will bow their knees to His sovereignty and declare His Lordship. They will speak it out loud. No one will be exempt. This will include every creature – in the physical realm and in the spiritual realm – including the greatest enemy of Jesus: Satan himself.

How wonderful it is for those – alive on the earth – who not only acknowledge His exalted position, but also let Him reign in their hearts as Lord of lords and King of kings. Imagine what that moment will be like for the ones who've lived in a humbled position and bowed to Him during their earthly existence. Pretty awesome, I'm sure.

Sum up today's lesson with **Ephesians 1:18-23**. Who is Jesus?

Give some thought to the *Finding Fullness of Joy* principle before writing it at the back of the book. How will you apply it to your life?

Finding Fullness of Joy:
Giving Jesus full reign of our bodies and bowing to His Lordship

Day 5
Working Out Your Salvation

Joyous Jewel

Continue to work out your salvation with fear and trembling.
Philippians 2:12

We live in the day of the health club. You're probably a member of a gym or have been at one time. Me too! The United States has approximately 30,000 health clubs with a total of 58 million memberships. That's a lot of people working out and a lot of muscle power. But here's a staggering statistic: about 80% of people will quit within a few months of joining a gym. We ask ourselves, "Why?" Why do people start off with a serious goal of getting healthy by exercising, and then just give up? Well, I think for most of those who quit it's because the work is strenuous. It's hard! They're just not willing to put in the effort it takes to see results. Here's my confession – I've quit more than once myself.

Sadly, many people approach their Christian life this way. They started off gung-ho with great enthusiasm for God's kingdom work, but when it became too time-consuming or too difficult, they quit. Do you know how many obstacles, hardships, and physical restraints the apostle Paul encountered in the years of ministry? More than we could imagine. Yet, he never quit! He never gave up! And today's exhortation tells us to do the same. As Christ-followers, it is our responsibility to work for God. Quitting the gym can be detrimental to our physical well-being, but quitting God's kingdom work will surely cause us to lose heavenly rewards **(1 Corinthians 3:14)**.

Write in your own words what Paul is telling us in **Philippians 2:12-13**. Try to be specific.

I would like to take this passage apart, so we might receive inspiration and help in our quest to follow God's mandate to work. I think you'll be encouraged through today's lesson and excited to move forward with God.

Paul offers three directives as we put our hands and feet into motion.

1. **Work with a trainer!**

What is the first word of **Philippians 2:12**?

The word *therefore* is a transition word connecting two thoughts. In this case, Paul wants us to know that what he's about to say is directly related to what he had just said. So, what did he say previously? Review **Philippians 2:5-9** and write down key words or phrases about Jesus.

Paul has never been one to beat around the bush. He says it matter-of-factly. This is what Jesus did for you, so you must do this. Sometimes, though, we don't know where to begin. This passage tells us to start with a *good* trainer. You and I know that a good trainer can make all the difference. One of the first things people do when joining a gym is meet with a personal trainer. This qualified trainer will help them get the most out of their workout. Of course, God doesn't expect us to work without being trained. He's provided us with the *best* trainer. Who is that?

First and foremost, we should follow Jesus' example. Imitate His ways. Get on mission with Him. What was He most passionate about? What did He give His time and energy to? How did He interact with others? How did He treat everyone – whether friend or foe?

What does Peter tell us in **1 Peter 2:21**?

How will you put this into practice?

Before we move forward, I must say that God also gives us plenty of other trainers as well. Paul said to **"follow my example, as I follow the example of Christ" (1 Corinthians 11:1)**. So find people that are following Jesus and then follow their example. Some of my mentors don't even know that I follow their example. But since they've made huge impressions upon my life, I choose to be inspired by them and I listen to what they have to say. Each of us should have good trainers to follow. By doing this, we will be more inclined to stay on the right pathway and not drift.

2. **Work hard!**

In relation to working hard, what does **Colossians 3:23** say?

According to **Colossians 1:28-29**, what was Paul's work and how did he work at it?

We read in **Proverbs 13:4** that **"the sluggard craves and gets nothing, but the desires of the diligent are fully satisfied."** In fact, the Bible has a lot to say about the one who is lazy. In her southern drawl, my grandma used to say, "Can't never did nothin'." We might say the same about laziness. It never accomplishes anything. But when we work hard for something and see results, we feel a sense of satisfaction. Here's the thing, though: we may never see results on this earth from the kingdom work we do. It's important we keep working, though, because the results will be revealed one day, that's for sure.

I heard a story of missionaries in Guatemala who served for years sharing the Gospel of Jesus Christ. During that time, they saw very few converts. They worked hard and then returned to the states. The missionaries that came after them immediately began to see fruit of the Gospel message. They witnessed tremendous growth in God's kingdom work. Imagine the rewards the first missionaries received in heaven for the work they did. This is a good reminder to keep on keeping on. And to always work hard because in the end, your effort *will* pay off.

In our key passage, **Philippians 2:12-13**, Paul gives us two features of our work:

- **Work out [your] salvation!**

Some people are confused by this passage and believe it's talking about working *for* salvation. Since the Bible tells us frankly that our salvation is given to us by God's grace alone **(Ephesians 2:8-9)**, then we can know that's not what this verse is referring to. This phrase *work out* actually means to work something to full completion. In ancient times, it meant "working a mine or working a field." In relation to a field, we know that we can never see the harvest if we don't work it. To see it to completion, we need to help nurture it by tilling the soil, weeding, and watering. Likewise, we must cooperate in the heavenly work to reap rewards.

Look back at **Philippians 2:12**. Whose salvation are we to work out?

What does this verse tell you about [your] salvation in relation to others?

We tend to look around and compare our call, our gifts, and our pathway to others. Well, there is no mistaking in this verse that each of us has unique purposes. Sometimes the call can be similar – there are many Bible teachers like myself – but the pathway is always different.

Recall the conversation between Jesus and Peter in **John 21:18-22**. What did Jesus tell Peter about *his* pathway versus John's?

Jesus had just told Peter what kind of death he would one day experience, and Peter knew exactly what Jesus was talking about. I'm sensing a twang of jealousy in Peter's heart toward his fellow disciple. Perhaps he was thinking, "Jesus always seems to single me out, but John is just about perfect. He seems to always do the right thing, but I'm always getting in trouble." In any case, Jesus tells Peter to not look at others but to only focus on himself.

We should build on our own relationship with Jesus, not someone else's. There is no need to copy others' gifts or ministries, because God has set you apart to uniqueness. If you are unsure what pathway He has for you, then ask Him. He loves when we ask. Remember this… comparing ourselves with others gives Satan a huge foothold – one we don't want him to have.

Now for the second feature of our work…

- **Work with fear and trembling!**

What does it mean to you that we should "work out our salvation with fear and trembling?"

The phrase *fear and trembling* doesn't mean that we are to be afraid of God or scared of what He will do if we don't live up to His standards. It means that we are to have a reverential awe and wonder of God. Our work should be done in a worshipful attitude because of who He is.

Explain this thought further from **1 Corinthians 10:31**?

Now, let's examine our final directive as we put our hands and feet to work…

3. **Work with divine power!**

According to **Philippians 2:13**, how can we do what God puts before us?

It's true that we often think of the "faith giants" as people with extraordinary power – supernatural abilities. If we were to list those biblical giants, I think the apostle Paul would be at or near the top of our list. He seemed to have great strength to carry out God's mission. But Paul refutes any belief that he stood apart.

What does Paul say about his arrival in Corinth in **1 Corinthians 2:1-5**? What does he give credit to for his abilities?

What kind of power resides in us **(Romans 8:11)**?

That is some power. In fact, I can't think of another power source stronger than the one that can raise Jesus from the dead. This is the Holy Spirit's work and He lives in each of us. That means that you and I can do exemplary things – unbelievable tasks for God. But here's what we should remember: *always* rely on the power of the Holy Spirit, not on your own strength. We will have much more impact and our work will reap grander rewards when everything we do is done through the power God has bestowed on us.

Review today's lesson and write down what God is speaking to you about. Then meditate on today's *Finding Fullness of Joy* principle as you write it down in the back of the book.

Finding Fullness of Joy
Remaining steadfast in God's kingdom work

1. LOGOS, *Word Studies in the New Testament.*
2. http://www.dictionary.com/browse/contention?s=t
3. http://www.gracevalley.org/sermon/selfish-ambition/
4. *Zondervan NIV Exhaustive Concordance* (Grand Rapids, MI: Zondervan Publishing Co.), 1563.
5. W. E. Vine, *Vines Complete Expository Dictionary* (Nashville, TN: Thomas Nelson, Inc.), 251

Week 4

Sweet Smelling Sacrifices

Day 1
Bright Lights in a Dark World
Day 2
Poured-out Life
Day 3
Indispensable Friend
Day 4
Partnering in the Work
Day 5
The Worth of a Servant

Jesus had many encounters with the Pharisees, a religious sect of Judaism. He often condemned them for their unholy behavior. He called them hypocrites. Their teaching was in complete contradiction to Jesus' teaching. The Pharisees gloated in the spotlight, while devaluing others. They puffed themselves up, as they put others down. They lived a lie and pushed people away from the truth. The Pharisees pointed to themselves, and at the same time, turned others away from God. Hence, the Pharisees and Jesus stood on opposite sides of the character fence. Jesus told the crowds that the Pharisees do not practice what they preach **(Matthew 23:3)**.

Sounds like the world we live in. A world that has become self-centered. This selfish behavior became really clear to me the other day when I was out driving. I noticed that people cut others off, ignore those trying to merge in, tailgate cars going slower than they are, block intersections, cut in front of people sitting in construction areas, and speed up to get a parking space as others wait. There seems to be no regard for others. This kind of greedy behavior happens in every arena, and even in the Church. Did you also know that the Bible condemns such behavior?

This week we will examine the manner of conduct Jesus honors. The kind the Bible praises. Paul uses word pictures and examples of others who exemplified noble living. He gets real with us as he invites us in to his own heart. He shows us what sacrifices are truly sweet to the Father – sacrifices the Father *loves* to breathe in. I believe we will be inspired this week in our quest to please our God.

Day 1
Bright Lights in a Dark World

Joyous Jewel
Shine like stars in the universe as you hold out the word of life. Philippians 2:15-16

Begin by reading our key passage, **Philippians 2:14-16**, and then write down your thoughts.

There's something magnificent about a star-lit night. I love going outside and gazing into the sky to see multitudes of bright luminescent stars. I'm sure you love it, too. It's amazing how some stars are brighter than others. All the stars point to the Creator of the Universe, but those bright ones seem to speak the loudest. Their sparkling gleam makes us gasp in wonder at the One who placed them in the sky and **"calls them each by name" (Psalm 147:4)**.

But here's the cool thing… in the pages of Scripture, the people of God are compared to the stars in the universe. Imagine that! And since we are like the stars, we were also created to shine. To shine for God. And it's our responsibility not to just shine, but to shine *brightly*. However, the reality is that a lot of God's stars are barely illuminating the darkness. Rather than lighting a pathway through the darkness, they just blend in with the world.

Describe the word picture in **Daniel 12:3**.

I believe Daniel reminds us that we shine brighter when we lead people to righteousness, to God. Something tells me that you, like me, want to shine so brightly that people pay attention. We want to be stars that reveal the God of the universe. Today's lesson will show us how we can shine brighter. I don't know about you, but I want to be like those bright stars that seem to illuminate the evening sky – the ones that point the way to my Creator.

I'm drawn to sunshine. I feel happy, healthy, and emotionally stable when the sun is out. The sun isn't the source of my contentment – Jesus is – but it sure helps. You know what I mean, don't you? There's more depression and sadness throughout the winter months than at other times of the year because the days are shorter, drearier, and darker during the winter. Light makes darkness disappear. Light illuminates our passageway and pierces through the night.

So to understand our role as lights, we need to get a little background information first. How does the apostle Paul describe the earth, based on **Philippians 2:15**?

Look around. Do you see the world as *crooked* and *depraved*? How?

By looking at the Greek rendering of these words, we get a deeper picture of the world we live in. The word *crooked* comes from the Greek word *skolios*. This is where the English word *scoliosis* comes from and means, "a curvature of the spine." In this passage, it refers to people who are morally perverse; in contrast to what is "good." They simply do not stand up straight. The Greek word for *depraved* is *diastrepho* and means, "they have turned away, or turned from the truth." [1]

I think these two words shed intense light into the condition of our world. Sin has invaded the earth and has therefore, darkened it. Truth, goodness, and morality are forms of light. Therefore, they are not at the core of the world because the world is dark. And people are still groping their way through the darkness waiting for the light to go on. Hence, there's only one light that can pierce through this darkness.

What is that light source, according to **John 1:6-9**?

Yes, Jesus came as a light to this world. But He is no longer here. His people are, though, and they were created to be the lights to shine in this darkened place. Imagine how much darkness would dissipate if believers shone as brightly as the brightest star in the night sky.

With that said, let's pull out three factors from our passage, **Philippians 2:14-16**, that will show us how to shine brighter:

Do not complain and argue!

Write your own definition to these words:

Complaining:

Arguing:

When non-believers hear Christians complaining and arguing, what do you think their first thoughts are?

Exactly! There is nothing that brings more dishonor to the kingdom of God than complaining and arguing. Yet, complaining and arguing have become a way of life for many of us. *The weather is horrible; it's awful the way I was treated; the leaders in the church aren't handling things correctly; no one understands; how can you believe that?* When we complain and argue, we are telling people that we believe God is doing a poor job and we could do a better job. Through this bad behavior, we diminish the sovereignty of God. Being a beacon for Jesus should help people find their way *out* of the darkness and *into* the light. But complaining and arguing doesn't help anyone, nor does it reveal the true character of God.

Look up the following verses. Instead of complaining and arguing, what are better ways to handle ourselves – ways that will help us to shine brighter?

Ephesians 4:29:

1 Thessalonians 5:18:

Ecclesiastes 10:12:

1 Thessalonians 5:11:

Colossians 3:16:

If we could learn to put into practice these principles, we would shine like stars in the universe and lead people out of the darkness and into the light of Christ.

How will you make these truths a reality in your life today?

Stay pure and blameless!

We may look at these words and think we just cannot live up to them because they seem to speak of living a life without sin. But we know that's impossible. So what do these words mean and what do they have to do with shining for Jesus?

The word *blameless* means to "not cause one to stumble." [2] And the word *pure* refers to moral and ethical purity. [3] Hence, we are to live clean innocent lives.

Based on these definitions, how do the following verses explain purity and blamelessness further?

2 Corinthians 8:21:

Proverbs 4:25-27:

Romans 14:13:

Proverbs 21:3:

       Paul says, **"Let us walk properly" (Romans 13:13 ESV)**. The Bible is the most beneficial book for the believer. Why? Because it's God's standard for Christian living. To walk properly as Paul says is to walk according to Scripture. Of course, we can't always do it right. We will fail sometimes, but it's our responsibility to try to live the way God instructs us to live.

       Here's a good reminder: the world is watching us. Do we get up and go to church on Sunday, but live just like the world during the week? Do we take time to help those in need, or do we disregard the people in our community? Do we fudge on our taxes? Do we lie when confronted with wrongdoing? Are we fighting with those who live differently? It is important we don't put a stumbling block in someone's way. A transformed life is an effective witness to the cause of Christ. Staying pure and blameless is one sure way to shine brightly for God.

       Reflect on this point. Is there some area of your life you need to change? Explain.

Hold out the word of life!

       This phrase *hold out* comes from the Greek word *epecho* and means, "to hold fast, give attention to, give heed to." [4] In the New Living Translation, this phrase is rendered *hold firmly*. It's also translated *holding forth* in the King James Version. One commentary said that holding forth is a translation of a Greek word used in secular documents of offering wine to a guest. It means, "to hold forth so as to offer." [5]

       I can't offer something to someone if it's not mine. I can offer my time to a friend, my attention to a sibling, my love to my husband, and even my beach condo to a family member. Those things belong to me. Jesus Christ – the word of life – also belongs to me. But this phrase tells me that I need to not only hold onto Him, but to also offer Him to others – to share the Gospel. The Gospel is the *only* light that can lead people out of darkness.

       How did this type of behavior affect the apostle Paul in **Philippians 2:16**?

       I hope today's lesson will help us all to be brighter stars in the universe. Seek to apply today's *Finding Fullness of Joy* principle and then record it at the back of the book.

Finding Fullness of Joy

Walk properly without complaining and arguing

Day 2
Poured Out Life

Joyous Jewel

But even if I am being poured out like a drink offering on the sacrifice and service coming from your faith, I am glad and rejoice with all of you. Philippians 2:17

We love stories of people who overcame great odds to accomplish amazing things. We're inspired by their determination and their giving-it-their-all mentality. We love successful endings to difficult beginnings. Two brothers fit this category: Wilbur and Orville Wright. When they were little, the spark to build a flying machine was ignited when their father came home from a trip and gave them a toy helicopter. From that time forward, the brothers worked hard to master vital aspects of the very first airplane. They literally poured out everything to see their dream come to fruition. Since then millions of people have benefitted from their hard work and perseverance.

But nothing inspires me more than hearing stories of people who have poured out everything for the cause of Christ. Their devotion, dedication, and humble service motivate me to remain faithful to my calling. From the moment Saul (the apostle Paul) had his Damascus Road experience and met Christ, he poured out his life for Jesus' mission. For thirty years, he remained steadfast and committed as he preached the Gospel, raised up fearless leaders, and equipped many believers in truth. And he did all this while facing intense opposition. Paul is one of my greatest heroes. I look forward to meeting him one day.

Read **Philippians 2:17-18**. How did Paul view his life?

The believers in Philippi would understand this phrase "being poured out as a drink offering" from a couple different viewpoints. In pagan cultures, people would take a vessel (often it was a glass of wine) and pour it out over their sacrifice. This was their way of saying, "I'm going all in." And in the Old Testament a drink offering was used as part of the sacrifice. It was an act of worship.

What does Numbers **15:5** and **7** reveal about drink offerings?

A drink offering is such a sweet aroma to God that when He breathes it in, He is so pleased. Therefore, imagine the pleasure Paul's sacrifice was to God. I want to imitate this *drink offering* so I, too, can please my Lord. I hope you do, too. But keep in mind that we *cannot* pour out what we don't have inside us. So we need to drink in before we can pour out.

Let's observe one story in the Bible that shows this in its fullness. From the following passages, how do you see Mary living this out?

Luke 10:38-42:

John 12:1-3:

I noticed two specific things in these passages: Jesus honored Mary for her "drinking in" *and* there was a sweet aroma that filled the place when Mary "poured out." With that said, we need to examine both aspects to get the most from our study. I trust that you and I will put a huge smile on Jesus' face with the sweet aroma coming from our drink offerings.

Drinking in!

We can learn a lot from the apostle Paul's prayers. The things he brings before God truly show his heart and what he wanted to see most in God's people. Read through the following prayers and write down what he longed to see.

Colossians 1:9:

Ephesians 3:14-19:

Philippians 1:9-11:

Did you notice that a common word in each of these prayers is *full*? Let's hone in on this. Fill in the blanks from the following verses…

Colossians 1:9: "…asking God to fill you with the _____ of his will through all _____ _____ and understanding."

Ephesians 3:19: "…that you may be filled to the _____ of all the fullness of God."

Philippians 1:11: "…filled with the _____ of _____ that comes through _____ _____" …

Summarize your findings in one or two sentences. What are we to be full of?

What is the word picture in **Psalm 23:5**?

A cup overflows when it can no longer hold what's being poured into it. It's so full that it just comes spilling over the rim. I believe this is what our lives should be like to be poured out as a drink offering. We need to keep drinking in the abundance Jesus offers us until there's nowhere else for all that beautiful stuff to go but out. Being a sponge is good, but only for a little while. Even sponges get full. And so it is with us.

From the following Scriptures, what kinds of things does God give to us in excess?

Lamentations 3:22:

Psalm 108:4:

Ephesians 1:3:

James 1:17:

God offers to us a wealth of incredible gifts, like truth, wisdom, discernment, love, knowledge, peace, patience, and faith. These are the heavenly gifts we need to keep drinking in. But here's what we sometimes forget: a cup cannot hold water when it's already filled up with mud. Peace cannot occupy a heart that's filled with fear. Love cannot coexist with hate. Truth cannot reside side-by-side with lies. Faith can never take the center of a heart that's replete with doubt.

Take a moment to ponder what's in your heart. Is it good stuff or bad stuff? Go before God and ask Him to show you what you may need to let go of so that your heart will be ready to receive what He wants to pour into it. Write down what He tells you and then write out your prayer.

Now, what will you drink in? And how often?

Pouring out!

According to **Philippians 2:17**, what was Paul's drink offering poured out on?

When we experience Christ to an exceedingly high degree, we become a drink offering. The New Testament writings show us that the apostle Paul was continually growing in his faith and striving to become more like Christ.

What was at the core of Paul's longing **(Philippians 3:7-10)**?

Not only was Paul smart and gifted, but he loved Jesus more than life itself. He's my role model. He should be yours, too. He didn't think of himself as better than others; he just wanted to know more about the One who died for him and offered him a brand-new life. He wanted to know God's character, how He worked, what was at the center of His thinking, and how all things work together. He longed to understand God's power, His love, His grace, His faithfulness, and His ways. Paul continually drank of the heavenly cup until it just poured out into others. He spent his time and his attention investing in the lives of others. That was his drink offering.

What made the apostle Paul glad, according to **Philippians 2:17**?

When you are committed to investing in the lives of others – when all you want is to see people grow in their relationship with Christ – then you know that your cup is so full it's overflowing, and you've become a drink offering. There's nothing that makes my heart rejoice more than seeing God's people learn truth and understand Scripture. I smile each time someone tells me how a Bible study changed their life or how a message ministered to their heart. When this happens, I know that I've become a drink offering poured out on the sacrifice and service of their faith. But keep in mind that we may not always know how we're impacting someone's life. We need to serve Jesus out of the overflow of what He's pouring into us, not to get accolades from people.

How are we to serve based on **Galatians 5:13**?

Remember that the pouring out is a result of the drinking in. Today's lesson is speaking to me. I know that I need to drink more. How about you? Write down what God is speaking to you about and then meditate on the *Finding Fullness of Joy* principle before writing it at the back of the book.

Finding Fullness of Joy

Pouring ourselves out as an offering for other believers

Day 3
Indispensable Friend

Joyous Jewel
I have no one else like him… Philippians 2:20

Living in the spotlight with huge demands put on you can be a lonely place to be, especially for those in ministry. The apostle Paul was the most well-known evangelist of the first century and was a busy man. But I don't think he would label himself lonely. It's clear from Scripture that he had lots of friends, acquaintances, and co-workers: Luke, Barnabas, Silas, and Priscilla and Aquilla were among some of his closest confidants. Today, however, we will look at another dear friend: *Timothy*. In Timothy, Paul had a friend, colleague, and trusted partner. We will quickly realize just how blessed Paul was to have Timothy by his side.

You may be tempted to ask yourself how you can find a friend like Timothy. But I want you to approach today's lesson from another angle. Ask yourself: "How can I be this kind of friend to someone?" When you become this kind of friend, you will then be an invaluable and indispensable asset to someone's life and ministry. And this will bring such joy to both of you.

Read **Philippians 2:19-24** and write down everything you learn about Timothy's relationship with Paul.

Timothy surely was indispensable – truly essential – to the apostle Paul's ministry. Paul's work was challenging to say the least. But I'm pretty sure that having Timothy by his side eased some of the weight he carried on his shoulders.

According to **James 2:23**, what was Abraham called?

This is the only place in Scripture where someone is called God's friend. That doesn't mean that God doesn't consider others His friend. I believe if we love Him, worship Him and obey Him like Abraham did, He calls us His friend, too. How would it make you feel to hear God call you His friend? Likewise, imagine being at the top of the apostle Paul's "friend" list. What an honor, huh? Well, Timothy had that spot. No matter what Paul was doing, where he was, or what ministry he was immersed in, he could always count on Timothy. Now that's what I call a true friend.

From our passage, **Philippians 2:19-24**, let's observe three characteristics of a priceless friend – the kind of friend Timothy was to Paul.

Like-minded!

Paul said about Timothy, **"I have no one else like him" (Philippians 2:20)**. It seemed that Timothy stood out from Paul's other friends. They were all important to him, but I'm thinking Paul might have referred to Timothy as his BFF. People can certainly challenge our joy, but the right kind of people can add to our joy. This is the kind of friend Timothy was to Paul. Something tells me that when Timothy was around, Paul felt pure joy. Not only were they best buddies, but they worked well together.

A like-minded person shares the same passions, beliefs and values as you. You may have different gifts that complement each other, and that's always a good thing. But at the end of the day, you're both headed in the same direction with the same goals. This is a *great* team.

What does the writer of Proverbs say about this kind of friend in **Proverbs 27:9**?

Is God calling you to stand beside someone, to help them? Write down what you'll do.

Attentive to others!

How did Paul describe what some people were doing to him in **Philippians 1:17**?

How did Timothy look at others in the church **(Philippians 2:20)**?

We know that Paul loved God's people. He writes to the church at Philippi: **"God can testify how I long for all of you with the affection of Christ Jesus" (Philippians 1:8)**. We have already mentioned how we live in a self-centered world. Sometimes I speak to people who only talk about themselves – they want me to know how they're doing and what's going on in their life, describing every detail. Now, I love hearing how others are doing, but sometimes they never ask me how I'm doing or what I've been up to. I often walk away wondering if they care about my situation. Imagine how those truly struggling feel when someone doesn't acknowledge them or ask them questions.

What is the law of Christ, according to **John 13:34**?

Look at **Galatians 6:2**. What is one sure way we can fulfill Christ's law?

The word *carry* comes from the Greek word *bastazo* and means, "to help, support, to take up, or to bear." One commentary says that to "bear one another's burdens, you are to assume those burdens in a willing, helpful, sympathetic way, even though the bearing may involve unpleasantness and heartache. [6]

Explain carrying others' burdens further by using **1 Thessalonians 5:14.**

This verse offers us a beautiful word picture of what it means to carry others' burdens. If I were to put it into my own words, I might say: we are to lovingly warn our brothers and sisters when they fall into sin, cheer them on when they're afraid or they don't think they can do it, try to ease the weight of those carrying heavy burdens, and wait patiently for God to move. How much easier it is to handle difficulties when we have someone who pays attention and comes along side of us. No doubt, Timothy demonstrated this marvelously. And this surely added to Paul's joy.

Do you know someone who is currently walking down a destructive path, or someone who has recently told you they are afraid to move forward, or someone whose burdens are heavy right now? If so, what will you do to help them? Write out your answer.

I must say this. Our kindness can easily be rejected. People often don't want help. It can make them uncomfortable, it can add to their guilt, or perhaps they don't see their need for help. So when this happens, pray that God would soften their heart and show them their need for help. Just don't give up.

Dependable!

Fill in the blank from **Philippians 2:22: "But you know that Timothy has _____ _____, because as a son with his father he has served with me in the work of the gospel."**

There's nothing like having a dependable friend. I've had some in my life that frequently cancelled the plans we set, always showed up late, and never followed through with their word. They just weren't dependable. I can tell you that the close friendship we once shared didn't last long. We all need dependability in our lives. Do you know someone who seems to always say, *I'll call, text, or email*, but they never do? Yeah, you know what I'm talking about, don't you?

Another word for dependable is *trustworthy*. Paul's mission was vital to the growth and the stability of the Church. He couldn't have done it by himself. What a blessing it was to have such a dependable and trustworthy friend by his side. Because of Timothy's consistency and faithfulness, Paul counted on him.

What did Paul say about Timothy in **1 Corinthians 4:17**?

What is Paul's instruction to Timothy in **2 Timothy 4:1-5**?

Paul spent considerable time pouring truth into Timothy. He was mentoring him to carry on the work when he was gone. Paul would die, but Timothy was to continue the work. He *trusted* Timothy. He counted on him. Paul wrote to Timothy these words: **"You have heard me teach things that have been confirmed by many reliable witnesses. Now teach these truths to other trustworthy people who will be able to pass them on to others"** (2 Timothy 2:2 NLT).

Oh, how the younger Christian generation needs to be trained in truth. They are often taught watered-down formulas of truth or they simply learn from the world because there isn't anyone to mentor them. I believe the corporate Church is failing to teach the younger Christians the whole unadulterated truth. The future leaders of the Church will need to understand that truth *is* truth. What God calls sin *is* sin. And God's Word is truth. Young people – as well as seasoned believers – often let their lifestyle influence truth. But we need to live and teach one thing: to let truth influence our lifestyle. In Timothy, Paul had a valuable confidant – he was like-minded, attentive, trustworthy, and dependable. Timothy would equip others with truth – the truth that was taught to him by the apostle Paul.

Do you do what you'll say you'll do? Are you someone others can trust? Would people call you dependable? Ponder these questions and write out how you can become a Timothy to someone in your life.

Timothy did not just have a vital place in Paul's ministry; he also secured a precious place in Paul's heart. Focus on today's *Finding Fullness of Joy* principle and write it at the back of the book.

Finding Fullness of Joy

Becoming a valuable asset to someone's life and ministry.

Day 4
Partnering in the Work

Joyous Jewel

For he longs for all of you and is distressed because you heard he was ill. Philippians 2:26

At the end of any movie is a list of credits; the names of those who played in the movie and the names of those involved with the movie. Most of them go unnoticed because they work behind the scenes to bring life to the big screen. Yet, their work is still important. Where would the movie be without the screen writer, the costume designer, the director, and the photographer? Each name may only be included in a list, but the movie would never make it without them.

In the Bible, we are familiar with those who stand out: Moses, David, Isaiah, Peter, John, Paul, and a slew of others. Without a doubt, they were true servants of the Most High God and treasured assets to God's kingdom purposes. But what about all the others? The ones who are mentioned very little or not at all? I believe that some of God's most valued servants are people we've never heard of. Their names may appear in just a couple verses, in a genealogical list, or may not appear at all.

Does this give you any indication of your kingdom work? What?

Today's character, *Epaphroditus*, is only mentioned in two sections of Scripture and both are in the book of Philippians. But we will soon find out how much of an asset he was to the apostle Paul's work and ministry.

Read **Philippians 2:25-30**. What do you learn about Epaphroditus?

What else does Paul tell us about Epaphroditus in **Philippians 4:18**?

Epaphroditus was from Philippi and was saved when Paul came to town and preached the gospel. Paul was in prison in Rome at the time of this letter, and it appears that when the church at Philippi wanted to send a gift to Paul, Epaphroditus either volunteered or was selected to deliver it. During his time in Rome, the apostle grew to love and appreciate him. He considered him a huge part of his ministry. While not much is written about him, Paul packs a lot of amazing credentials into a small space. I believe you and I will come to realize that the Church needs more people like Epaphroditus. He is surely someone we should strive to emulate.

With **Philippians 2:25-30** before us, let's examine three amazing qualities about this beloved helper to Paul.

Epaphroditus was...

Solid!

What does Paul tell us about Epaphroditus in **Philippians 2:25**? List every title.

Based on this verse, why do you think the apostle Paul loved Epaphroditus?

We should strive to be solid Christians and Epaphroditus shows us exactly how to do that. Paul gives him three titles:

Brother

How should a brother act, according to **Proverbs 27:10** and **Hebrews 13:1**?

How can a brother love his fellow "Christian" siblings **(James 2:14-16)**?

It's easy to say we love our fellow brothers and sisters in the Lord, but demonstrating it is something altogether different. We should look for those with needs and then step up to the plate and help. I believe this is one solid Christian trait often overlooked or neglected. Remember, we're a family and family takes care of each other. Let's love the way we should love.

Is there someone you are called to love today? How will you show your love to them?

Fellow worker

What does it mean to you that Epaphroditus was a fellow worker of the apostle Paul?

When I was a youth leader many years ago, we took the kids canoeing every summer. I remember a few times when we were going against the current. It was hard. We would paddle and paddle and never seem to make headway. That's the same with working for the kingdom of God. Christians often work against each other, rather than with each other. It's important for the body of Christ to work together – partnering with one other. If we don't work together, then it will become much more difficult to overcome the challenges. But partnering together will advance the gospel and God's work will go forth with much more power and influence.

What is one benefit of working together, according to **Proverbs 27:17**?

Fellow soldier

In our lifetime, we will fight for certain things we believe in. We will speak up when our kids are being mistreated, we will attend school board meetings when we don't agree on the curriculum taught, we will write letters to congressmen when we want to make a statement. I know I've been there but sometimes I feel all alone in my fight. I feel like I'm the only one wielding the sword. You know what I'm talking about, don't you? But when there are others who fight with me, the battle doesn't seem so difficult.

I wonder if Paul had this in mind when he wrote that Epaphroditus was a fellow soldier. Epaphroditus wasn't just sitting in the bleachers cheering Paul on in the fight (like so many others), but he got in the game. He picked up the sword of the Spirit, prayed, and defended what had been entrusted to them. Therefore, Paul didn't feel alone. In the battle, it's nice to have someone fighting with you.

Look up **Luke 10:19**. Should we be afraid of the fight? Explain.

How will you get in the fight and stand beside your brother or sister in Christ?

As a Christian, all three of these qualities are important. Many believers are strong in one or two of them – not all three. But when we're strong in *all* of them, our Christianity is solid – balanced.

Epaphroditus was...

Sensitive!

How did Epaphroditus show his sensitive spirit from **Philippians 2:26-28**?

Epaphroditus was sensitive to his brothers and sisters at home and he was also sensitive to the apostle Paul. He was deeply concerned for the welfare of others, even though he was suffering himself. He had been in Rome longer than he had anticipated and couldn't wait to get home to see how his Christian family was doing.

He would be the kind of person always checking up on you. He would visit you in the hospital, bring a meal to you when you're sick, send a card when you're having a difficult time, and pray unceasingly for you.

What did Paul write earlier in his letter in **Philippians 2:4**?

I love when someone gives me an example or a visual. I'm much more inclined to understand what they're saying or remember it if I can picture it. Paul gave a visual here. After speaking into their hearts this truth, he offered them an example of someone who was living that way. And here's the cool part: the example was of someone they knew personally. Paul wanted the Philippian believers to be as grateful for their brother in Christ as he was.

Relate **Romans 12:16-21** to being sensitive to others.

Paul says, **"In doing this, you will heap burning coals on his head" (Romans 12:20)**. In Bible times, a person had to keep a hearth fire burning all the time for cooking and warmth. If it went out, they would go to their neighbors for live coals of fire. They would then carry them in a container on their head back to their house. The one who supplied the live coals was meeting a desperate need of theirs and showing an outstanding act of kindness. [7] Hence, when we are sensitive to others' needs and help them, like Epaphroditus did for Paul, we show them a great kindness. God is surely pleased with this kind of service.

How will you display this sensitive spirit to someone?

Epaphroditus was…

Sacrificing!

How was Epaphroditus sacrificing **(Philippians 2:30)**?

Epaphroditus volunteered for a long trip. He traveled from Philippi to Rome, a journey of 800 miles. We can drive that trip in about fifteen hours, so imagine how long it took in the first century without modern luxuries? And when he was in Rome he became sick and almost died. He sacrificed his own desires and comforts for others.

The word *sacrifice* means to "surrender or give up." When it comes to giving up our own desires, comforts, or plans for someone else, that often goes against our flesh. Most of us think of ourselves first. We certainly wouldn't want to travel 800 miles to hand a gift to someone. Paul tells us that our sacrifice is one sure way to worship Him **(Romans 12:1)**.

Review today's lesson. Write down what God is speaking to you about. Then read today's *Finding Fullness of Joy* principle before writing it in the back of your book.

Finding Fullness of Joy
Living a life of sacrifice and service to others

Day 5

The Worth of a Servant

Joyous Jewel

Welcome him in the Lord with great joy, and honor men like him. Philippians 2:29

We have all sorts of ways to honor people: a graduation party for the grad, a welcome home ceremony for the decorated soldier, a plaque for the one who's gone, a family get-together for a mom on Mother's Day, a dinner for the retiree, and a celebration for the talented athlete. When people do something notable, perform some service, or to keep their memory alive, we love to honor them. I've been on both ends and it's always rewarding, whether I'm the one being honored, or I have the opportunity to honor someone. People are a blessing from the Lord and we should honor those in our life.

The Bible talks a lot about honoring others. Look up the following Scriptures and write down who we should honor.

Ephesians 6:2:

1 Peter 2:17:

1 Timothy 5:17:

Romans 12:10:

According to **1 Corinthians 6:20**, who else are we to honor and how are we do it?

Is it time you honored your parents, a friend, a co-worker, a pastor, or someone who's always there for you? How have you been honoring God today? Just think about this as we move forward.

We will conclude our lesson this week talking about honoring others, simply because Paul talks about it in Philippians 2. But the kind of person we are to honor might not be who we think. Certainly not the kind of person the world would celebrate. In referring to Epaphroditus, what did Paul tell the Philippian church in **Philippians 2:29**?

Review what you learned about Epaphroditus **(Philippians 2:25-30)**. Write down words that describe him.

Does this give you any idea of the kind of person who truly honors God? What would those characteristics be?

Epaphroditus wasn't rich, famous, powerful, or distinguished. Those are the things the world honors, but not God. Epaphroditus was a humble servant, serving Paul and the Philippian church. He put others' needs above his own. He partnered with his home church and the apostle Paul, risking his life for the sake of the Gospel. Epaphroditus would carry Paul's letter back with him and they were told to give him a huge welcoming party. They needed to honor him. Beautiful, huh?

Look up **Psalm 112**. Based on this chapter, write down what qualities bring honor to God and what the rewards are for living in such a way.

Brings honor to God	Rewards

From **Psalm 112:7**, fill in the blank:

He will have no fear of bad news; _____

_____.

I had the opportunity of sharing my dad's life at his funeral quite a few years ago. Looking out at his beloved family and friends who had gathered, I recalled the story I had heard many times over the years. When my parents were young with four small daughters, my dad was making some mistakes and in jeopardy of losing everything. In desperation, he called a pastor friend. And on this pastor's living room floor, my dad surrendered his life to the Lord. This was the beginning of a brand-new life for my dad and it changed the dynamics of our family, as we began to go to church together as a family. After the funeral service, the pastor that was with my dad on that day said to my mom, "Jack never did waver." Hence, he remained steadfast the rest of his life.

I have a friend who grew up not knowing God and by the time she was a teenager, she had decided she didn't believe in God. She became an atheist – an outspoken atheist. She was angry and bewildered about life. Then sitting at a Billy Graham crusade, she became restless and uncomfortable. So she walked out before the invitation was finished. In the parking lot, she could still hear Dr. Graham's voice booming over the loud speakers, and that's when she fell to the ground in repentance. Her life was dramatically changed that day. She is now sold out for Jesus and her faith has remained steadfast.

God surely honors the one who stands in awe of Him, who lives a righteous life, follows His commands, gives freely, remains steadfast, and the one who humbles himself before God and others. Epaphroditus fits these criteria. We don't know much else about him, but we do know why Paul respected him so much and why he told the church folk to honor men like him.

As a Church, we should follow this instruction and honor those who humbly serve. These are people we may not recognize so we may have to look for them. Do you know anyone like Epaphroditus? Someone who has a servant heart? Someone who is in the background always ready to serve? Who comes to your mind? And how can you honor them?

Slowly read **2 Peter 1:5-9**. List the honorable qualities we should strive for. Circle any you need to do further research on.

What will happen if we do these things **(2 Peter 1:10-11)**?

We don't know what that welcome will be like, but I'm pretty sure it's far grander than any honorable ceremony, dinner, or party we'll participate in on this earth. This is God's way of honoring those who have lived a godly, humble life – those who lived the way He told them to live. And I'm fairly certain you would like to have this rich welcome when you get to Heaven. I know I do. Therefore, I will try to live like Epaphroditus. I will aim to please God rather than people. I will make every effort to serve even if it goes against my human flesh. How about you? Will you do it, too?

What is God speaking to you about today? How will you apply His truth to your life?

Reflect on the *Finding Fullness of Joy* principle and then write it at the back of the book.

Finding Fullness of Joy
Place in high esteem those with servant hearts.

1. *Zondervan NIV Exhaustive Concordance* (Grand Rapids, MI: Zondervan Publishing Co.), 1541.
2. *Zondervan NIV Exhaustive Concordance* (Grand Rapids, MI: Zondervan Publishing Co.), 1532.
3. W. E. Vine, *Vines Complete Expository Dictionary* (Nashville, TN: Thomas Nelson, Inc.), 498.
4. *Zondervan NIV Exhaustive Concordance* (Grand Rapids, MI: Zondervan Publishing Co.), 1551.
5. LOGOS, *Wuest's Word Studies in the Greek New Testament*.
6. Ibid.
7. LOGOS, *Wuest's Word Studies in the Greek New Testament*.

Week 5

Admirable Ambition

Day 1
A Good Safeguard

Day 2
Swapping our Confidence

Day 3
Infinite Value

Day 4
Pressing On

Day 5
Eager Anticipation

Sometimes we get stuck. Stuck in the mundane. Stuck in the past. Stuck in our circumstances. Stuck in the middle. We want new. We want exciting. We want joy. We want to move beyond our past mistakes or our current situation. Instead, it often feels like we're stuck in the quicksand with no way out. We want to get unstuck – to move forward. But pulling our self out is another thing all together.

Staying in the same bad situation too long can... damage our confidence, lower our self-esteem, drain our energy, keep us from success, ravage our health, distort our clarity, cause us to fall into discouragement, make us feel distant from God, *and* rob us of joy. Sometimes we're stuck, and we don't even know it. Other times we know it but feel helpless to do anything about it. I've been there! You probably have too!

Something tells me that the people to whom Paul was writing may have also felt stuck. Maybe they were hanging onto legalism, still trying to live under the Old Testament law, rather than enjoy the freedom in Christ Jesus. Maybe they couldn't move beyond their former sin or past missteps. Perhaps they just couldn't get over their hurts and move into God's redeeming forgiveness. Whatever was going on within the church at Philippi, Paul was on a mission to help them press on. Our lesson this week will offer us practical ways to get unstuck and to experience even greater joy. I believe each of us will find this week's lesson inspiring and relevant to our lives.

Day 1
A Good Safeguard

Joyous Jewel

Finally, my brothers, rejoice in the Lord! It is no trouble for me to write the same things to you again, and it is a safeguard for you. Philippians 3:1

People offer us all kinds of advice when we're struggling. They might tell us to stay positive, hang in there, pray, or to be encouraged. They tell us to keep focused on God's Word and rest in Him. Of course, these are all good things. But when we're immersed in a huge struggle, we often get frustrated at their advice because we think they haven't walked in our shoes. They don't know what we're going through. So, we can easily tune them out.

We have heard Paul say repeatedly in the book of Philippians to be joyful. But here's the best part: the apostle Paul was speaking from experience. He certainly had every right to *not* be joyful. His circumstances were horrible. The battle strenuous. The pain unbearable. Yet, he was joyful. Imagine that! The way I look at it is if the apostle Paul can be joyful in the midst of his difficulties, then I surely can too.

Paul doesn't just tell us to be joyful; he left principles to help us attain a joyful attitude. At the conclusion of every lesson, I hope you're discovering the *Finding Fullness of Joy* principle and then writing them at the back of the book. Joy *is* possible no matter what's going on. Paul doesn't just speak about it; he demonstrates it as well.

Read **Philippians 3:1-3** and write down the theme of these verses.

If you're a parent, you know there are always things that bear repeating because we want our kids to get it. *Don't go near the street. Brush your teeth. Don't talk to strangers. Eat your vegetables. Get your homework done. Say please and thank you.* When we're young, we think our parents sound like broken records, but guaranteed those things they repeated often, we remembered. And we're probably saying the same things to our kids. On the same note, there are some things repeatedly said in Scripture. Perhaps God is saying, "I hope you pay attention to this. I want you to get it."

In the book of Philippians, Paul repeats a phrase several times. What is it, according to **Philippians 3:1**?

Why is this phrase important to his readers?

In this first verse of **Philippians 3**, we learn two important things about joy:

Joy is...

Anchored in Christ!

Fill in the blanks from **Philippians 3:1**:

"Finally, my brothers, rejoice _____ _____ _____."

I heard it said that *joy* was Paul's outlook because Jesus was Paul's *uplook*. Don't you love it? When reading the New Testament, there is no doubt that Paul was anchored in Christ. And this anchor is what offered Paul such joy in the midst of daunting circumstances and the ability to tell others to keep rejoicing. Read the following story and explain how Paul's joy burst through when others were discouraged.

Acts 27:13-44:

An anchor gives a boat stability and keeps it from drifting. In today's world, it's easy to drift into dangerous territory. It's easy to come loose from the stability we once had. Instability can lead us to improper actions. And if we're not careful, we can lead others astray. We want joy. We want contentment in the middle of the storm. Paul shows us that it is possible, but here's the thing: real joy is *anchored in Christ.*

The other day I was talking to my mom about some people who have been fighting and not speaking to each other. Both sides have been hurt by the other. My mom said, "It's a God problem." In other words, if they sought a relationship with Jesus, then they wouldn't be acting this way. I couldn't agree more. Obviously, they are lowering the wrong anchor into the water – anchors that are not strong enough to keep their boat from drifting. Jesus Christ is the *only* anchor that can keep us stable.

Let me ask you. What is the anchor you're clinging to? If it's not Jesus, will you swap anchors? How?

Joy is...

A Safeguard for us!

Based on **Philippians 3:1**, why do you think Paul telling them to rejoice was a safeguard?

When we're in a safe place, we're content and satisfied. When our souls are at peace, our actions reflect that. Joy is certainly a safe place for believers to be. Why? Because joy keeps us from lashing out at people and falling into discouragement. It helps us to forgive the wrongs done against us, and it keeps our relationships strong. When we're joyful, we can simply rise above anything in our way. Joy surely is a haven of safety and a place we should be drawn to.

Now keep in mind what Paul is saying about joy – it's our anchor and our safeguard – because he's about to give us two specific reasons why joy is important.

Joy keeps us...

From wrong actions!

What is Paul's warning in **Philippians 3:2**?

How does Paul describe these people?

Scholars believe Paul is talking about men called Judaizers. They were troublemakers in the early church. These were strict Jewish believers who instructed the Gentiles to submit to Jewish rules before being saved. Let's quickly look at the three things he tells us about them:

The Judaizers were...

Dogs! These dogs are not the cute little puppies that are our pets. No, they were wild dogs – scavengers that carry dangerous infections. Judaizers were teaching false doctrine and telling believers to adhere to it.

Men who do evil! They taught that works are necessary for salvation. But these works are evil because they are done in the flesh and not in the Spirit.

Mutilators of the flesh! The word *mutilator* is another word for circumcision. They taught that circumcision (as in the Old Testament) – a cutting away of the flesh – needed to be a part of their salvation.

The apostle Paul confronted Peter on this very issue **(Galatians 2:14)** because he was teaching the same thing as the Judaizers. Paul at one time had been a strict Jewish leader living by rules and regulations. But when Jesus saved him and then trained him in the way of grace, Paul learned that grace was enough for salvation **(Galatians 2:16)**. Hence, Jesus did all the work for us at the cross. Works should be a part of our faith **(James 2:17)**, but they are never a part of our salvation **(Ephesians 2:8-9)**.

What do you think Judaizers look like in today's Church?

Of the Christians serving and working in the Church, there are many working in the flesh. They simply move forward in their own strength and *they* hold onto the glory rather than offer it to God. They look for praise. They love when people put them on a pedestal. They love sitting in a place of exultation. They love getting pats on the back. These people are no different than the Judaizers because they are adding their own works to the law of grace. And when we add anything to grace, it negates its significance.

Joy keeps us...

From putting confidence in the flesh!

Explain true Christians based on **Philippians 3:3**.

What is the difference between Judaizers (false Christians) and true Christians?

Using Jesus' parable in **Luke 18:9-14**, what are the characteristics of both the false Christian and the true Christian?

In your own estimation, how does a true Christian look? And why is it important we take heed to these descriptions?

The word *flesh* in **Philippians 3:3** means our "old nature." The nature that was ours before we were sealed in Christ. Paul describes our old sinful nature with words like: immorality, impurity, idolatry, jealousy, strife, disputes **(Galatians 5:19-21)**. I see a lot of these things still prevalent in Christians, the people of the church. There are so many sinful things going on within the church – fighting, bickering, back-stabbing, coveting, and substituting things for God. Why do you think this is so? Perhaps it's because we're not content in our life, in our relationship with Christ?

Think about this last question before answering. Why do you think *joy* can keep us from wrong actions and from putting confidence in the flesh?

Ponder the *Finding Fullness of Joy* principle and then write it at the back of the book.

Finding Fullness of Joy
Anchor yourself in Christ

Day 2
Swapping our Confidence

Joyous Jewel

But whatever was to my profit I now consider it loss for the sake of Christ. Philippians 3:7

Imagine giving up the throne to a country and the luxuries of a palace to live in a mud hut in the slums of India. Or forfeiting the Olympic games to run a city marathon with few spectators. Or turning down a lucrative physician job in New York to help the sick in Papua, New Guinea. Or giving up a pastorate position at a large mega church for an assistant pastorate at a small country church with barely fifty in attendance on Sunday mornings. It's hard to imagine, isn't it?

Well, that's exactly what happened when Paul had an encounter with Jesus. Not only was his spirit changed forever, but his circumstances changed as well. Paul went from receiving praise from men to being persecuted for his faith; from a place of prestige to a place of disregard; from prominence to unimportance; and from a comfortable lifestyle to unpleasant circumstances. Paul also gave up a good wage to sometimes go without food and shelter. And here's the remarkable thing: the apostle Paul did all this willingly.

Have you had an encounter with Christ? Did it change your life? Write down what happened and what you gave up for Him.

Meeting Jesus Christ *should* change everything for us. Your story may not be as dramatic as Paul's, but an encounter with Jesus should bring us to a place of total allegiance – a place where we give it all to Him. Today's lesson will inspire us as we listen to what exactly happened to Paul.

Read Paul's candid words in **Philippians 3:3-7** and then list his former credentials.

We know modern-day credentials, but we can be a little confused on the things that once defined Paul. So let me break them down for you. Read on…

Circumcised on the 8th day: Converts to Judaism were circumcised in maturity and Ishmaelites were circumcised in the thirteenth year. One born into Judaism was circumcised at 8 days old. Paul had a fabulous birthright. He was Jewish royalty.

Of the people of Israel: Paul was native to the land, not a transplant. He was born and raised in Israel.

Of the tribe of Benjamin: The tribe of Benjamin was a highly respected tribe in Israel – the tribe where Jerusalem was. The Benjaminite's had remained loyal to David and they formed with Judah the foundation for the restored nation after the captivities.

Hebrew of Hebrews: Paul was the son of Hebrew parents who had retained their Hebrew language and customs, in contrast to the Hellenized Jews who read the Old Testament in the Greek language.

Pharisee: The Pharisees were an influential sect of Judaism. They were known for their emphasis on personal piety, their acceptance of oral tradition in addition to the written Law, and their teaching that Jews should observe all the laws. The Pharisees were the strictest sect of religious Judaism **(Acts 26:5)**.

Zealous persecutor of the church: A Pharisee must defend lies and Jesus was a deceiver to them. Paul defended his duties by persecuting the followers of Jesus. He could boast of his faithfulness to the Jewish religion plus his zeal in persecuting the Church.

Righteous, faultless: Paul believed he followed the Pharisaic law perfectly. He held to the Orthodox doctrine and tried to fulfill the religious duties faithfully. When measured by the righteousness of the Law, Paul was blameless. He observed the laws and the traditions.

What else does Paul tell you about his former days in **Galatians 1:13-14**?

Last week I took my mom to the doctor for a check-up. They discovered something in her breathing and then sent us immediately to the cardiologist. When the cardiologist noticed who our doctor was, he said, "Dr. Greene is one of the smart ones." I think he was saying that Dr. Greene is the cream of the crop – probably someone who graduated at the top of her class. My mom and I walked out glad that we go to a "smart" doctor.

From what Paul writes about his former days, it seems he was also at the top of his class – advancing faster than any of those his own age. His peers might tell us, "Yeah, Paul graduated Suma Cum Laude. He was one of the smart ones."

Sum up in your own words Paul's former credentials.

Write down your credentials. What have you accomplished? Did you graduate with honors? Have you received a college degree? A book contract? A recognition for something? A corporate job? What names and titles do you hold?

Do these things bring you great joy? Feelings of worth? A sense of pride? Be honest and explain what they do for you, for your self-worth.

What picture does **Luke 18:10-14** paint about the Pharisees?

What does Jesus say about the Pharisees in **Matthew 23:1-7**?

Jesus had many things to say about the Pharisees – none of them good. From the two passages above, we might label the Pharisees with words like: judgmental, hypocritical, prideful, showy, pompous, and self-righteous. They walked through town and sat in places of honor with their heads held high, rarely lowering it to notice the needs of the common folk. They looked down their righteous noses at the lower class of people as they thought they were better than everyone else. Oh, they felt so good about their status, their accomplishments, and their place of honor in God's dynasty. And, of course, sin was reserved for everyone else.

This is probably a perfect picture of the apostle Paul before his conversion experience. Not only was he a Pharisee, but he was of the elite class of spiritual leaders. He had everything at his command. He was moving up the Pharisaic ladder quickly and traveling all over to bring the hated Christians down. He was proud of who he was. He had accomplished much, and he gained a great deal of respect among his colleagues and the spiritual hierarchy within the Jewish community. But then… he had a glorious encounter with Jesus.

Let's travel back to that day – the day everything changed for Paul. Read **Acts 9:1-9** and summarize.

Considering the man he once was, how do you think this experience changed him? What do you think He recognized about Jesus and himself?

Perhaps Paul beheld the power, the authority, and the sovereignty of the Son of God. Without a doubt, his eyes were opened as he saw Jesus and heard His voice. In the blink of an eye, Paul was *completely* transformed. The old was gone; the new had come. Paul was in the presence of the Almighty One who sits on the throne. And the light was so bright that his eyes were blinded. Imagine that!

A personal encounter with Jesus would surely change anyone, especially if they had been a great enemy of His. Paul thought that Jesus' followers were crazy people, believing in a lie. How could they believe that Jesus was the promised Messiah? I mean, He came from Nazareth of all places **(John 1:46)**. His teachings were absurd, unorthodox. And rise from the dead? Come on! His followers needed to be stopped before they succeeded at proselytizing more vulnerable souls. But now for the first time, Paul understood. They weren't crazy. They had had an encounter with the Living One. The One who really did come back to life.

How do you know that everything changed for Paul based on **Philippians 3:7**?

Paul swapped his confidence. At one time, he had put great stock in his earthly credentials, feeling pretty good about himself and all he had accomplished. He must have relied on those things quite often. But once he encountered Jesus Christ, his earthly accreditation meant nothing. NOTHING! From that point forward, it was all about Jesus. At one time his measuring stick was the world and the Law, but then his measuring stick took on a whole new dimension. Everything was measured next to Jesus. And Paul's confidence shifted.

What truth is found in **Proverbs 3:26**?

I believe we need to, from time to time, have a fresh encounter with Jesus. Because it's in this place where our hearts are transformed – set on fire for Jesus. And this is when our confidence shifts from self-centeredness to Christ-centeredness. So let me ask: Have you seen Him lately? Have you heard His voice? Spend some time right now with Jesus. Record what He shows you.

Now ponder the *Finding Fullness of Joy* principle and then write it at the back of the book.

Finding Fullness of Joy

Find your value, your self-worth in Jesus Christ and Him alone

Day 3
Infinite Value

Joyous Jewel

I want to know Christ. Philippians 3:10

When we give up something important to us, it's often for something better. One summer when I was in college, I gave up working and making money to go on a mission trip to Guatemala. A learning experience I will never forget! I've also given up vacation time to be a camp counselor, the single life for the married life, social activities for college work, one job for another job, and a ministry position for another. In all these cases, I gained something better by giving up what was important to me. You may have a similar story.

In our previous lesson, we learned what had been important to Paul before his conversion – the credentials he at one time had put his confidence in. Initially, we noticed that he went from royalty to commoner so to speak. He gave up popularity for persecution, prosperity for poverty, and power for prison. While it's hard to imagine, today we'll see exactly what he gained. And it's something so much better.

Slowly read **Philippians 3:8-11**. Write down the things Paul considered a gain.

What are some things you consider valuable in your life? Be specific.

Most of us would certainly consider our family, our heritage, our friends, our jobs, our health, our church, and our faith as valuable. Each of those things is important to us. They have certainly molded us into who we are. Paul may have had a similar list. Today's lesson though, discloses what would have occupied his #1 slot: *Jesus Christ*. Paul is about to show us that he gained far more than what he lost – infinite value.

Fill in the blanks from **Philippians 3:8**:

What is more, I consider everything a loss compared to the _____ _____ of knowing Christ Jesus my Lord, for whose sake I have lost all things.

This phrase *surpassing greatness* is referring to something so valuable – far more valuable than anything else. Nothing in life could compare to Jesus Christ. Hence, Paul lost his religion, but he gained Christ. I believe that you and I need to lose some things to really gain Christ. Maybe we

104

need to lose our theological ideas – the belief system we've stuffed into a box. Maybe we need to lose the self-made stringent rules we live by. Or the guilt weighing on our shoulders because we think we don't measure up to other believers. Perhaps we need to lose our ministry position for a time, so we might gain Christ. I think Jesus often gets pushed behind the walls we've built up – the walls labeled religion, doctrine, tradition, and ritualism.

Is there something you need to lose before you can *really* gain Christ? Write it down with your prayer for deliverance.

Is there something specific you want to gain in Christ? Something you have felt at a loss with? Well, in this passage, Paul gives us four specific things he gained in Christ. Things of *infinite value* he sought hard after. I'm certain that if you and I seek after these things too, with great resolution, we will surely gain Christ. Let's discover what they were…

1. Knowledge of Christ (verse 8)!

The Greek word for *knowledge* is *gnosis* and means, "knowledge gained from first-hand (personal) experience." [1] This is the knowledge gained through having a personal intimate relationship with Jesus Christ. It's not just knowing *about* Him. It's *knowing* Him.

Write your own definitions of the following phrases:

Knowing about Him:

Knowing Him:

I'm sure you realize that it's not the same thing to know *about* someone than to really know them. One person I consider a great mentor is Kay Arthur: author, Bible teacher, and president of Precept Ministries. For three years I sat under her expository teaching of God's Word. And it was during that time I began to sense the call on my life – to empower believers in solid truth. Hence, I know a lot about Kay Arthur… she's passionate about God's Word, she has been faithful to her calling, she has impacted thousands just like myself, and she is a former missionary. But I *don't* know what kinds of food she likes, what she does in her spare time, how she thinks, and what her deep passions are right now. The only way I can know those things is to spend quality with her.

The same with Jesus. We can know a lot about Him: He was born in Bethlehem, He was a great teacher, He had many enemies, He had twelve disciples, He was put to death and rose from the dead on the third day. Most people know these things. But what is at the center of His heart? What is He most passionate about? What does He want from His followers? How does He respond to His enemies? Here's the thing… We *can* know Him. If we spend time with Him, He will reveal these things to us. And I believe each of us wants to know Him just like Paul did. There really is nothing that compares to knowing Jesus Christ. But here's what we need to remember: spending time with Him requires sacrifice and commitment.

Are you willing to make the sacrifice and commitment it will take for more intimate knowledge of Him? How will you do it? What's your prayer right now?

2. Righteousness of Christ (verse 9)!

Based on **Philippians 3:9**, where does righteousness come from and how do we attain it?

The word *righteous* means "a right standing with God." So what Paul is saying is that at one time, he tried, but failed, to become right with God by keeping the Law. But his faith in Jesus Christ changed all that because Jesus exchanged his sin and short comings for His complete righteousness. So for us, it's important to know that no amount of law keeping, self-improvement, discipline, or Christian service can make us right with God. Righteousness comes from God and is attained by faith in Jesus. That's all. This is freedom at its best.

What does it mean to you to be right with God?

As God's righteous, what is our position **(Ephesians 2:4-7)**?

How does Jesus see us **(2 Corinthians 5:17)**?

We often see our mistakes, scars, imperfections, and sin. It's easy to focus on these things. But the Bible is clear on one specific thing: once we are made righteous in Him through our faith, Jesus sees us as new creations and offers us a brand-new position – a position in the heavenly realms. He *only* sees His righteousness in us. Therefore, we need to stop living under the bondage of guilt because of what we've done or what sin we've committed. Our faith in Jesus Christ has made us right with Him.

How do you see the righteousness of Christ as a gain?

3. Fellowship of Christ (verse 10)!

Write out **Philippians 3:10.**

The Greek word for *fellowship* is *koinonia* and means, "the close association between persons, emphasizing what is common between them; participation, sharing." [2] Hence, the apostle Paul wanted to walk alongside Christ and share the same things: power, suffering, and death. Imagine that! We can certainly understand wanting the same power that raised Jesus from the dead. We long to have more power to do greater things for God. But the same suffering and the same death? Those two are a little more difficult. Yet, we just might share these things without even knowing. Write down the truth in each of the following verses:

Romans 8:11:

1 Peter 4:12:

2 Corinthians 4:11:

Let's now look at a couple other verses that explain why this fellowship is worthy.

Matthew 5:11:

1 Peter 4:13-14:

I think what believers forget is that we have been given the same power that raised Jesus from the dead. There is not a greater power than that and it was given to us just because we put our faith in Jesus. I think Paul knew the magnitude of his calling and he didn't want to do it without the greatest power. We should want that, too. And well, suffering, is par for the course. Believers who are out on the front lines for Jesus and speaking truth *will* be persecuted because the world, and sometimes the Church, hates Christ's message **(John 15:18-19)**. Satan comes after fully-devoted Christians more than others, because they're a threat to him. But if we persevere, we'll be blessed and honored. I know I want God's blessing. I'm sure you do too.

How do you see the fellowship of Christ as a gain?

4. New life with Christ (verse 11)!

What does **Philippians 3:11** tell you about death?

Oh yes, we will one day be resurrected from this place to a new home that awaits us.

What are your thoughts from today's lesson? Now ponder the *Finding Fullness of Joy* principle and write it at the back of the book.

Finding Fullness of Joy

Losing what's important to us to gain Christ

Day 3
Pressing On

Joyous Jewel

I press on toward the goal to win the prize. Philippians 3:14

Imagine you signed up for a race. A difficult race through the mountains of Colorado. So you hire a trainer who puts you through grueling exercises to get you ready. For months, you've trained hard. On the day of the race, you sign in and get your jersey number. Along with many others, you take your place at the starting block. The gun goes off and you begin with a steady jog. Eventually you're running faster. It starts pouring, but you keep running. The pavement is slick, and you fall. But nothing will stop you, so you pick yourself up, brush the gravel off your knees, and keep running. After what seems like an eternity, the finish line is in sight. Huffing and puffing, you muster all your strength and step over the line. Completely exhausted and covered in sweat, you raise your hands in victory. You made it. Oh, how proud you are.

Well my friend, there's a race Paul talks about in his writings. A race each of us are called to participate in. It's never easy. The terrain is difficult sometimes and the weather isn't always predictable. We will stumble along the way and maybe want to quit. But the end isn't too far off. The finish line is in sight. And those who make it will be awarded a glorious prize. It's not about coming in first, second, or fifth. It's about persevering to the end. It's about not giving up. It's about keeping on no matter how tired you are. This race is surely worth every drop of sweat.

Read **Philippians 3:12-16** and summarize.

The good news is that God doesn't expect us to run without help. He offers us a wonderful trainer: the apostle Paul. Listen up because our trainer is about to give us five valuable pieces of advice as we run in this race.

1. The race is still on!

What does Paul say about completion in **Philippians 3:12**?

Some believers get to a place where they feel satisfied with their spiritual attainments. So they stop learning and growing. And they stop ministering to the people around them. They simply become complacent in growth or retire from God's work. Friends, let me remind you that the race is still in full mode for us because we are still here. Therefore, complacency and retirement are not options. If Paul said he hadn't reached perfection yet, then we haven't either.

According to the following Scriptures, what are we to be doing?

Ephesians 4:15:

1 Peter 2:2:

2 Peter 3:18:

After I graduated from Bible College, I thought I was done learning. I really thought I didn't need further education in God's Word. Not out of pride, but out of ignorance. Then I was invited to a Precepts Bible study, which began a brand-new adventure in the study of God's Word. And I haven't stopped growing since. Our growth is essential to the stamina we'll have in the race. It will help us persevere until the end.

How much time do you spend learning God's Word? Answer honestly.

2. Keep going!

Fill in the blank from **Philippians 3:12: ...but I _____ to take hold of that for which Christ Jesus took hold of me.**

The Greek word for *press on* is *dioko* and has the meaning of striving and pressing on to a goal with intensity. Hence, Paul is telling us that as he runs, he is concentrating on the goal, the finish line. No doubt, this is true of every serious athlete since the race can be burdensome. Concentration will help us to stay on the right pathway and will keep us diligent in our stride to reach the finish line.

According to **2 Timothy 2:5**, how are we to compete?

Athletes are often disqualified or lose rewards because they cheat or fail to follow the rules. It really is a shame, but they must follow the rules. The same is true in this athletic race. God has given us His Word to live by and it's important we don't negate it. If we don't follow His rules, we can lose rewards

Based on **1 Corinthians 3:10-15**, what are some rules we must follow to get rewards? What happens if we don't follow His rules?

Are you following the athletic rules? Explain.

We've been talking about concentration. What is one sure way we can concentrate as we run **(Hebrews 12:2)**?

3. Don't look back!

Based on **Philippians 3:13**, what direction did Paul NOT go?

According to **Hebrews 12:1**, what are we to do to make the race easier?

An athlete bent on winning never looks back because he might surrender time, stumble, or lose sight of the goal ahead of him. Imagine if Paul looked back. He had been steeped in religion, he was filled with fury, and he had made plenty of mistakes, including persecuting the Church. If he looked back, those things would have surely hindered him from moving forward.

As a Bible teacher, I get negative comments from time to time. Not long ago, I received an accusatory message from a lady. I was devastated! But after spending time before God, I realized her remarks were unwarranted and they had no solid base. I knew I had to put these thoughts behind me or I could lose my footing. I could have easily stumbled or given up completely. There are many things that can hinder us. But Paul is telling us what he did with those things: he left them behind. There's not a better place for them. We will run faster, have more endurance, and will be less likely to fall if we just don't look back.

Is there something hindering you? What is it? How will you leave it behind?

4. Focus on the finish line!

As Paul raced, what direction was his focus **(Philippians 3:13-14)**?

Paul was certainly an athlete running in God's marathon. Give a description of why Paul was a successful Christian athlete based on **1 Corinthians 9:24-27**.

We spend a lot of time working toward temporal things. We run hard after what we want. We exert a ton of energy toward stuff that won't last. The message Paul is bringing before us in this passage of Scripture is that we need to run even harder toward the prize awaiting us because it will last for all of eternity. What do the following phrases mean to you?

I do not run like a man running aimlessly:

I do not fight like a man beating the air:

God has put His purpose in each of us. He's put before us a goal. He's given us a fabulous reason why we should run toward His finish line. Because His crown will be far grander than any earthly reward we've ever received. If we keep our focus on the finish line and the prize given to those who cross over, the race won't seem so grueling.

One job I never coveted was translating the Bible. Sometimes missionaries had to start from scratch because they were sent to a group of people with no written language. But I couldn't imagine the tedious work they endured day in and day out translating the Bible into another language. Why would they do this? Because they were commissioned by God, so they ran tirelessly.

What has God called you to do? Are you doing it aimlessly or with purpose?

5. Run together!

What does Paul call for in **Philippians 3:15-16**?

Relate these verses to what Paul said earlier in **Philippians 2:1-4**.

One message Paul preached often was *unity*. I believe what he's saying here in Philippians is that as we run, it's better to run together. Let me remind you that just because you're on the track running, doesn't necessarily mean you are running side-by-side with other believers. I've witnessed great division in the Church. There's so much tension and separation over petty differences. If we allow these things to continue, it only weakens our stance. There is certainly strength in running together.

Review each point from today's lesson. What is God speaking to you about? Then ponder today's *Finding Fullness of Joy* principle and write it in the back of the book.

Finding Fullness of Joy
Keep running with the finish line in sight

Day 5
Eager Anticipation

Joyous Jewel
But our citizenship is in heaven. And we eagerly await a Savior from there, the Lord Jesus Christ. Philippians 3:20

I've traveled to many different countries. Each place brings new adventures with unique features. I loved the biblical landmarks in Israel, the historical charm in Italy, the majestic beauty in Greece, the ancient ruins in Mexico, the cultural differences in Guyana, and the pristine coastline in Antigua. But I must say that while I look forward to going abroad, I'm always ready to come home at the end of the trip because I feel most at home in *my* country – the place of my citizenship. Maybe it's because I'm just ready for some good ole' American cuisine and the comforts of speaking my own language. Either way, I love coming home.

The apostle Paul traveled to many different places preaching the gospel and equipping believers. But his earthly citizenship was in Rome – a place of esteem in that day. And while he could have held his head up high and boasted of his prominent citizenship, he was far more excited about another place of citizenship – a place he loved to talk about. A place far grander than Rome. A place where he would one day live permanently. Oh, how he was looking forward to this place. Let's conclude this week by observing what he had to say about this place of great anticipation.

First, what does Paul reveal about himself in **2 Corinthians 12:1-4**?

What does he tell us about this paradise?

Something tells me that Paul loved to talk about his awaited home because he, at one time, caught a glimpse of this majestic place. And it was so awesome he couldn't even talk about it. Imagine that!

What word of encouragement did Paul give in **Colossians 3:1-2**?

I wonder if God allowed Paul a peak into heaven, so he could encourage his readers to keep their eyes on it, especially since life was unbearable at times for the believers.

Summarize **Philippians 3:17-21**.

Citizens of a specific country are not just inhabitants; they are also entitled to the country's privileges. As a citizen of the United States of America, we are entitled to many freedoms and rights. As Christians, we have dual citizenship. Our earthly citizenship and our heavenly citizenship. Imagine the privileges we are entitled to as citizens of heaven. Surely nothing on this earth can compare to *those* benefits. In our passage today, **Philippians 3:17-21**, we learn some amazing facts about our heavenly citizenship. Follow me as we unfold them…

Citizens of heaven are…

Part of a family!

How does Paul refer to the Philippians believers in **Philippians 3:17**?

What qualifies us to be a part of God's family, according to **John 1:12-13**?

I recently talked to two siblings who have become estranged. They're both mad at each other and rarely speak. I reminded them that they are sisters and always will be. I encouraged them to work things out because in the end, when their friends are gone, they will only have each other. The truth of the matter is that most earthly families are broken and dysfunctional. And some don't have an earthly family connection. But the good news is that believers in Jesus are members of another family – a family with awesome perks and a perfect Father.

Oftentimes our brothers and sisters in Christ are closer to us than our biological sisters and brothers. But with family membership comes great responsibility. We should take care of each other, stand beside one another in the good times and the bad times, and love each other. We should support our Christian brothers and sisters through prayer and by putting their needs above our own.

A citizen's birth certificate is made valid by the registrar's seal. What makes your heavenly birth certificate valid, according to **Ephesians 2:13**?

The blood of Jesus can never be erased and will never fade away. Time doesn't weaken the seal; rather it strengthens it. When you acknowledged Jesus as your Savior, His blood was poured out over you. His blood is our protection and safety. And it authenticates our family membership.

Are you happy for this family membership? Tell God.

How will you take responsibility as a member of God's family?

Citizens of heaven are…

Surrounded by pretenders!

List the things Paul says about these pretenders in **Philippians 3:18-19**.

Just because someone says they're a Christian doesn't make them one. Just because we hear people pray in Jesus' name or talk the Christian lingo, doesn't necessarily mean they are members of our heavenly family. Pretenders sit among us, walk beside us, and partner with us. They fool many. We need to be careful who we trust because a pretender can take us down the same destructive path they're on. Paul tells us that they are enemies of the cross of Christ.

First, the apostle Paul reveals their destination.

Destruction!

Explain this destination further using **2 Thessalonians 1:8-9**.

Anyone who is an enemy of the cross of Christ will be forever separated from Jesus. It's not what I say; it's what God says. People have a hard time thinking that God would do this, so they choose to believe *only* in His love, mercy and grace, among other good things. The writer of Hebrews says, **"The Lord will judge his people" (Hebrews 10:30)**. So if we believe the whole Bible is the inspired Word of God, then we must believe in the justice of our God.

Next, Paul offers three ways we can pick pretenders out.

- *Their god is their stomach!*

They worship their fleshly desires and appetites. Paul writes about these people: **"For such people are not serving our Lord Christ, but their own appetites. By smooth talk and flattery they deceive the minds of naïve people" (Romans 16:18).**

- *Their glory is in their shame!*

Their morals and values are so distorted, they boast about things they should be ashamed of, like sexual perversion, abortion, and lifestyles contrary to the Word of God.

- *Their mind is on earthly things!*

They live as though this life is all there is. Their minds are focused on what the world offers – what will satisfy their own thirst for power, money, and fame.

Have you picked out a pretender? What have you seen and what will you do?

Now Paul quickly changes gears in this passage and turns his attention to two positive things about our citizenship. I hope you're getting more excited about your family inheritance.

Citizens of heaven are…

Eagerly awaiting their Savior!

What are believers struggling against **(Ephesians 6:12)**?

The world we live in may be different in many ways than the world the Philippian believers were immersed in, but the passage above exposes the war that has been raging in the spiritual realm throughout history. Therefore, we struggle in a lot of the same ways as Paul's audiences back in the day. Since the moment Satan landed on this earth, he's been at war with God. We only see little snippets, but it's surely powerful. I believe Paul is telling us how he was able to keep going with joy in the midst of the war – by eagerly anticipating his Savior. By waiting expectantly. Paul's main instruction in the book of Philippians is to "look ahead." And he was doing that by thinking about the moment he would look upon his Savior.

Let me ask you. Where is your attention focused? Are you disillusioned by all the mounting problems? Or are you eagerly awaiting your Savior, who promises to come back for you? Write down what you will do to change what you focus your attention on.

Citizens of heaven are…

Going to be transformed!

How will we be transformed, according to **Philippians 3:21**?

Hallelujah! We get to trade in our weak and frail body for a brand-new one. In fact, our new body will be like Christ's glorious body. I can't wait. How about you? Side note: if you want to learn more about this transformation, consider working through my Bible study, *The Bride of Christ*. In that study, we spend considerable time discussing the transformation process.

Review each point from today's lesson. What is God speaking to you about? Then ponder today's *Finding Fullness of Joy* principle and write it in the back of the book.

Finding Fullness of Joy

Keep your eyes focused on the home awaiting us

1. http://biblehub.com/greek/1108.htm
2. *Zondervan NIV Exhaustive Concordance* (Grand Rapids, MI: Zondervan Publishing Co.), 1565.

Week 6

Peace and Contentment

Day 1
Staying True to the Lord

Day 2
Worry Less, Pray More

Day 3
The Power of our Thoughts

Day 4
Learning to be Content

Day 5
Beautiful Offerings

I know I don't have to tell you what a crazy, mixed-up world we live in. My 83-year-old mom often says that there is no place in this world for her. I know what she means. This world is not the same world she grew up in. It's not the same world I grew up in either. And it's getting scarier by the day. Our spirits are troubled by the immorality, pornography, adultery, abortion, and drug and alcohol abuse. Not to mention the magnitude of suicide. We cringe at how materialism, consumerism and greed have defined the American dream.

Unethical leaders, killing babies, and the pursuit of power have become the norm. We cannot wrap our minds around what professors are teaching and the lies students are embracing. And then, of course, the false teaching that pervades the Church is very worrisome. It seems that every day, we witness violent acts in our country and around the world. Scary! Christianity is under attack! Our future hangs in the balance! No wonder *fear* has gripped our hearts. We want peace and contentment but wonder if it's even possible.

Well, we conclude our Bible study this week with a powerful teaching about peace and contentment. Paul wants us to know that these things *are* possible no matter what's going on around us. This week we add more principles to our already-growing list. Hang with me as we draw our Bible study and the book of Philippians to a close. I trust God has truly ministered to your heart through this amazing study. Now, let's move forward with the apostle Paul.

Day 1
Staying True to the Lord

Joyous Jewel
Rejoice in the Lord always. I will say it again: Rejoice! Philippians 4:4

One of the final miracles Jesus did (besides His own resurrection) was the raising up of Lazarus from the dead in John 11. Imagine being in the crowd on this day when Jesus, standing outside the tomb, gave a loud shout and called him back to life again. No doubt, Jesus saved the best for last. Of course, every miracle was spectacular. But this one, well… it was a glorious ending to a mighty compelling ministry. Scripture doesn't tell us, but I'm certain many people trusted in Jesus on this day – maybe townspeople, relatives of Lazarus, curious folks, and staunch religious leaders. Oh, how I wish I could have witnessed this miracle.

Often, we need to stay until the very end because that's when it gets *really* good. I'm glad you've stayed with the apostle Paul through the whole letter to the Philippians. He would tell you how glad he is too. He just might say to us, "Hang tight because it's about to get really good." Paul isn't going to pull any punches with the culmination of his letter. He will get right down to brass tacks and offer us more valuable principles that, when applied, can help us to live a life of true joy. And he will bring us closer in for the unveiling.

Begin by reading **Philippian 4:1-5**. What is the basic theme of these verses?

Paul seems to always have one main objective on his mind: a healthy church. He spends considerable time in his writings addressing problems that were causing havoc and dividing the church. The church cannot function properly or be a bright light in a dark world if it's unhealthy. I think we should learn what makes a healthy church.

Today's passage covers five components of a healthy church.

A healthy church is comprised of:

Love and respect for each other!

Fill in the blanks from **Philippians 4:1**:

Therefore, my brothers, you whom I _____ and _____ for, my _____ and _____...

Based on the blanks, how did the apostle Paul view the people of this church?

118

The church should be a haven for the hurting, the wounded, and the lost. What I mean is that the church should draw people in, not chase them away. Our church needs to help people find Christ. With that said, I guess we should ask what attracts people into the church? Well, I will tell you that fighting, division, competition, and hate will keep people at a distance and disillusioned. In contrast, though, *love* and *respect* are strong, alluring magnets.

According to the following verses, what is the responsibility of the church?

Hebrews 10:24-25:

Romans 12:10-13:

John 13:34-35:

The apostle Paul set a powerful precedent for the church. He had been away from the people for some time and he longed to be in their presence. He thought of them often. His heart filled with joy whenever he pictured this group of believers. And while he would get a heavenly crown one day, he considered *them* his crown. They were all the reward he needed.

Will you set a precedent like Paul? How?

A firm stance!

What exhortation did Paul give in **Philippians 4:1**?

Have you noticed a trend of unstableness in the church? How?

What important piece of theology is declared in **Hebrews 13:8**?

We live in the time that's often referred to as the New Age. This isn't just a religious belief system, but it's a term widely used to include all facets of life. Our world has adopted new thought systems, which focus on religious tolerance and moral diversity. In short, this belief system teaches to follow ethics rather than a moral standard (i.e. the Bible), live to please self, and to be tolerant (or have sympathy toward) religions, lifestyles, and philosophies we may not agree with. I'm sure you realize that this teaching goes against Christianity, that states that Jesus is the only way. And the Bible is surely the standard believers are to live by.

But here's the scary part: this teaching has not just infiltrated our country and the world, but it has also penetrated the Church. Multitudes of Christians are adopting this dangerous teaching as their own. Considering this, let's ponder **Hebrews 13:8** again, **"Jesus Christ is the same**

yesterday, today, and forever." That would mean that Jesus' teaching, character, and position have *never* changed. Jesus confronted sin. Jesus loved the sinner but spoke truth. Jesus told us to live to bring glory to Him and taught us to live righteously. Jesus' theology and this New Age theology stand on opposite ends of the spectrum.

What does Paul's exhortation to *stand firm* mean to you? Should we bend to accommodate the world's ideas? How will you stand firm?

Working out relationship differences!

What's the dilemma in the Philippian church, according to **Philippians 4:2-3**?

Review **Philippians 4:2-3** again and write down everything you learn about Euodia and Syntyche.

It's important to note that these women were believers and prominent members of the church at Philippi. They may have been deaconesses. At one time, they had been valuable assets to Paul's ministry and probably good friends. No doubt, Paul loved them both. But somewhere along the way, they had a falling out, a disagreement. Hence, they were not getting along. We know that unresolved conflict breeds all things negative: discouragement, anger, bitterness, and oftentimes nasty words. Splits in churches, failed ministries, divorces, and a breakdown in relationships, usually starts with a disagreement. A disagreement that is never fixed.

Did Paul expect these two to work it out by themselves? Explain.

Obviously, Paul didn't want this disagreement to cause further damage and threaten the stability of the church. So he enlisted the help of others in the church. *Help them get along.* People are often afraid to get involved, but Paul shows us that it's okay to step in and help.

What is the admonition in **Colossians 3:13-14**?

Are you in disagreement with someone? Write out what the disagreement is about and how you can work out your differences?

Joyful attitudes!

Write out **Philippians 4:4.**

I love that Paul repeated it. *In case you didn't hear me, let me say it again: Rejoice!* I wonder if there were a few smirks in the audience when this part of the letter was read. I wonder if some turned to their neighbor and said, "I think Paul wants us to get it." Well, maybe we should pay attention too.

We've talked a lot about joy in this letter, so let me ask: why do you think having a joyful attitude is crucial for a healthy church? Think about this before answering.

Gentleness!

What is the plea in **Philippians 4:5**?

Being gentle means to have a mild or kind nature. Oh, how important this is in the framework of any relationship or institution, especially the church. I've said many times that people are hurt more inside the church than outside. Perhaps that's why Paul wrote this. The opposite of gentle would be harsh, cruel, rough, callous, merciless. It's sad to say but when people get upset at others, they often speak out of their emotions, and you and I know that's never a good thing.

I remember one time my husband and I were turning left into a restaurant. The traffic was heavy, and another driver pulled around us and turned in front of us. My husband was angry, to say the least. He honked all the way into the parking lot, and I had to stop him from getting out of the car to give the other driver a piece of his mind. I reminded him of the problem with road rage in today's world. But this is more common than we would think. Gentleness has flown out the window.

What does **Titus 3:2** say?

I don't read in this verse that gentleness is for any specific time. No! We need to be gentle *always*. **Proverbs 15:1** says, **"A gentle answer turns away wrath, but a harsh word stirs up anger."** This verse explains why gentleness is vital to a healthy church.

We need to find a way to deal with people with gentleness. How will you do this?

Reflect on the *Finding Fullness of Joy* principle and then write it at the back of the book.

Finding Fullness of Joy

Work out your differences with love, joy and gentleness.

Day 2
Worry Less, Pray More

Joyous Jewel

Do not be anxious about anything, but in everything . . . present your requests to God. Philippians 4:6

Begin today by writing out **Philippians 4:6-7**.

Today we approach one of the most popular and quoted passages in the Bible, **Philippians 4:6-7**. I know I've recited it, pondered it, and pulled out the principles from these two verses many times in my life. So then the question becomes: Why do we seem to gravitate toward this passage? Well, I believe it can be summed up with a short sentence: *anxiety is one of our greatest struggles*. I know it's been a huge problem for me over the years. It's probably been for you too.

Anxiety (worry) has many root causes: stress, genetics, physical, chemical imbalance, traumatic event, or life's circumstances. Hence, anxiety is very real and attacks the weakest and the strongest. Believers are not immune. In fact, believers may be more at risk because of the enemy that pursues us. In my *Wilderness Wanderings Bible study*, I wrote a detailed account of my struggle with anxiety, fear and panic attacks.

The Greek word for *anxious* in **Philippians 4:6** is *merimnao* and means "to be troubled with cares." [1] Here's an interesting tidbit: the root of this word means "to divide, to separate." [2] Pastor Skip Heitzig says that this means to "divide the mind – that anxiety is when your mind is divided between legitimate thoughts and destructive thoughts. Anxiety takes your mind in two different directions."

Have you noticed a correlation between anxiety and your thoughts? How?

Think of a time that worry took over your thoughts. Can you think of anything good that came from worrying? Exactly what did it do for you?

We may ask ourselves: Does worrying help me feel better? Give me peace? Fix the situation? Offer me hope? Help me to sleep better at night? Your answer is probably the same as mine: No. But it's true, we worry and fret about many things. I wonder what was making the people of Philippi anxious. Maybe the persecution abounding, the stress of balancing family and church life, or perhaps it was looking into an unknown future. As Paul heard about their anxiety, he knew he could help them overcome it through biblical principles. The passage before us today reminds us that *any* anxiety can be overcome. Stay with me as we discover some valuable principles that can help us be free from the chains of anxiety.

The New King James Version Bible translates **Philippians 4:6** this way, **"Be anxious for nothing"** and can be rendered "not even one thing." [3] Hence, there isn't one thing we should worry about. That's strong language, don't you think?

Thankfully the apostle Paul gives us a prescription to help us on our journey to overcoming worry and attaining peace.

Write out the prescription to handle worry from **Philippians 4:6**.

So what does this mean? It simply means that we are to worry about nothing but pray about everything. This is convicting my heart. Do I pray about everything? Hardly! But I have made a commitment to try. There's not a better antidote to worry than prayer. When we bring our troubles to God, He takes them from us. Lifts the weight right off our shoulders.

According to **Philippians 4:6**, what three words are used to describe right praying?

_____ _____ _____

Let's look at each of these words individually as I'm sure they will give us deeper insight into this passage. The word *prayer* is the general word for making requests known to the Lord. It carries the idea of adoration, devotion, and worship. [4]

What do you learn about God from **1 Chronicles 29:11**?

Based on this verse, do you think God can take care of your troubles? How?

Of course, He can! He's God! Since we're talking about prayer, I do believe that each of us should spend quality time alone with God daily. Shut the noise out and come away with Him. I love the morning time; you may enjoy the nighttime better. But let me encourage you to devote a specific time each day to come into God presence. While we should pray throughout the day, we can hear His voice more clearly when we're alone. Worship is saying back to God what He has already said. I love to focus on His character, His attributes, and His power. I say out loud verses like **1 Chronicles 29:11**. By doing this, I'm reminding myself that God is very capable of helping me in my struggle. Sometimes we just need that reminder. Instead of worrying, worship!

Find a verse or passage about God and pray it back to Him. What does it say to you?

The word *petition* is also translated *supplication* in the New King James Version Bible. This word means "an earnest sharing of our needs and problems." [5] Hence, we are to pray wholehearted and sincere prayers.

What does Peter tell us to do in **1 Peter 5:7**?

The word *cast* means "to throw." I think sometimes we believe God doesn't care about our struggles and He's too busy to deal with our stuff. Nothing could be further from the truth. He voluntarily took the nails for your problems. By His wounds we are healed **(Isaiah 53:5)**. With this information before us, we should unload our hearts to God, the good things and the not-so-good things. Tell Him your troubles, so He may comfort you. Tell Him your joys, so He may smile with you. Tell Him your pain, so He may ease it. Tell Him about the wounds in your heart, so He may heal them. Bring before Him your thoughts, so He may cleanse them. Let Him know of the pride that's threatening to undo you and the temptation that has captured your heart. We need to cast our burdens, rather than carry them.

What do you need to cast before Jesus right now? Write out your prayer.

The third word is *thanksgiving*. Sometimes our problems overshadow the blessings in our life. When we're immersed in struggles, we often forget the good things God has done for us. We gripe and complain, wallow in self-pity, or get discouraged and frustrated. I believe this passage tells us that learning to be thankful can reverse all those negative things we're focused on. Let's do a quick Bible lesson on being thankful. Write out your findings from the following verses:

1 Chronicles 16:34:

1 Thessalonians 5:18:

Colossians 3:17:

Colossians 4:2:

Psalm 100:4:

Summarize your findings. What did you learn about thanksgiving? Why should we always be thankful?

How will you make thanksgiving a part of your day?

Now recap **Philippians 4:6**. What is God speaking to you about?

The book of Philippians is full of incredible principles that, when applied, produce wonderful solutions. Throughout our study, we've been writing *joyful* principles down. Today, we've been learning principles that bring about something else.

What does earnest prayer do for us based on **Philippians 4:7**?

Do you want peace right now? Do you believe it's possible no matter what? How do you know? Ponder these questions and then write your response.

How does **Isaiah 26:3** and **Philippians 4:6-7** correlate with one another? How can we attain peace?

Peace is the absence of fear and anxiety. Jesus demonstrated this all-encompassing peace when he stretched out His hand over the water and the storm ceased **(Matthew 8:23-27)**. The world and our circumstances can be in total chaos, but we can have peace. This kind of peace **"transcends all understanding."** The world doesn't understand it, but we can surely experience it. This peace is *only* possible by prayer and petition with thanksgiving. Peace is a major thoroughfare to abundant joy.

Write out the formula to peace in **Matthew 11:28-29**?

Ponder today's lesson. What will you do right now? Will you cast your cares at Jesus' feet and seek after peace? Write out how you'll do it.

Meditate on the *Finding Fullness of Joy* principle and write it at the back of the book.

Finding Fullness of Joy

Pray about everything and be thankful

Day 3
The Power of our Thoughts

Joyous Jewel
If anything is excellent or praiseworthy, think about such things. Philippians 4:8

We live in a world where people say that truth is relative; there are no absolutes. *Whatever my truth is might be different than your truth.* A generation has arisen where feelings trump truth. College professors are drilling this nonsense into young impressionable minds. And believe it or not, pastors driven by power, money, and notoriety are preaching it from the pulpit. One popular pastor said, "I don't need a book to prop up my faith." The apostle Paul would cringe at such heretical teaching since he spent thirty years defending truth – God's truth.

In our previous passage, we learned that one of the secrets to overcoming anxiety is prayer. We should cast our cares rather than carry them and replace worry with worship. As we continue in Philippians 4, we learn that Paul has more to say about how to overcome anxiety. In fact, he's about to give us another key that truly unlocks the *peace* door. And it all has to do with truth. Don't tune out now because if you want fullness of joy, then you need today's lesson.

Let's begin by looking at a couple verses that will shed light on our topic. Write down what you learn.

Isaiah 26:3:

Romans 8:6:

And now ponder **Proverbs 23:7** in the New King James Version translation: **"For as he thinks in his heart, so is he."**

Based on your reading, what do you discover about the mind?

Basically, we learn that good thoughts produce good works and bad thoughts produce bad works. Consequently, our peace and joy (or lack thereof) is directly related to what we think about – the stuff we put into our minds. Therefore, it's imperative we become intent on putting good things into our minds. Paul addresses this in his letter to the Philippians.

Summarize **Philippians 4:8-9**.

In this passage, Paul offers us a list of good things we should think about. I've listed each of them with a short definition. Next to each one, write down what kinds of things they might encompass.

True (correspond to the teaching of God's Word):

Noble (moral excellence):

Right (conform to God's standards):

Pure (free from the taint of sin; moral purity):

Lovely (beautiful, attractive – like generosity, kindness, compassion, forgiveness):

Admirable (things that give Christians a good reputation and a good name – like integrity, honesty):

Excellent (things that are virtuous, honorable, and good):

Praiseworthy (anything worth commending to others):

Explain why you think we should give more weight to these things than negative things.

The *mind* is a powerful tool and is often at the core of our struggles – our bondage. Our mind is also a target for Satan and the one place he knows he can conquer and use for his evil intentions. I don't know what chains you are bound up with, but I struggled for years with intense fear and deep insecurities. And my mind became a breeding ground for lies that held me captive. Did you know that worry, doubt, confusion, fear, anger, and feelings of condemnation are usually birthed in our minds? These things surely steel our joy and peace.

In light of our passage, carefully consider **2 Corinthians 10:3-5**. What are we exhorted to do with our thoughts?

What thoughts do you need to take captive to make them obedient to Christ? Write out your prayer of surrender.

What does Jesus tell us about Satan in **John 8:44**?

What does James tell us about our Father in heaven **(James 1:17)**?

Satan loves to whisper into our ears, but he always tells us things that are not true – lies. He looks for those times we're most vulnerable, like when we're upset, when we've been hurt, or when we're stressed out. He knows that it's then we're most likely to believe him. But remember this… if what we're believing is against Scripture, then it's not from God (because God only tells us good things). And those lies will lead us to move in ways that contradict the way we should act as God's ambassadors. And you and I know that nothing good ever comes from those kinds of actions – it always ends badly.

Let's look at four principles that will help us conquer negative thoughts.

Replace negative thoughts with positive ones!

We need to be conscious of our thoughts throughout the day. Maybe write down the negative ones and then find a verse or promise from Scripture to replace it. For example, you may believe you can't do something (maybe you're not qualified enough, trained properly, or not as creative as someone else). You could play **Philippians 4:13** in your head, **"I can do all things through Christ who strengthens me."** Do this with every negative thought.

Pour truth into your mind!

Since Satan is the father of lies and his language is lying, then the only thing that will stop him is truth. David was often tortured by negative thoughts when his enemies surrounded him. He said, **"I think of you through the watches of the night" (Psalm 63:6)**. David shows us how important it is to saturate our minds with truth. Truth and lies cannot coexist. And it's important to remember that TRUTH *always* prevails.

Speak God's Word out loud!

Satan cannot hear our thoughts, but he can hear what we say. When Jesus was being tempted in the desert, He proclaimed the Word out loud **(Matthew 4:1-11)** and the devil finally fled. I cannot tell you how many times I have paced in my house reciting God's Holy Word out loud during a struggle. God's Word is authoritative and reigns above all else. It's true that Satan will flee *every time* at the sound of God's Word.

Obey God!

If we obey God, then we aren't obeying the devil. Obeying God will pummel Satan's evil tactics right into the ground. David writes: **"The precepts of the LORD are right, giving joy to the heart" (Psalm 19:8)**. Obeying God is certainly an avenue for greater joy.

Look up **Romans 12:2**. With this verse in mind, review all four principles. Which one is speaking to you the most? How will you put it into practice in your thought life right now?

The apostle Paul concludes his thought process with **Philippians 4:9: Whatever you have learned or received or heard from me, or seen in me – put it into practice. And the God of peace will be with you.** I ask you, what have you learned from Paul? What specific truths stand out to you right now?

Let me clarify something: Paul isn't puffed up with pride when he says such a thing. He's simply saying that he walks in truth and we should seek to do the same. Paul is a beautiful picture of what a mentor should look like. He never compromised truth because the world was changing. It's sad, but so many have compromised. Recently I was talking to a friend who was struggling with a huge family issue. She went to three Christian counselors and none of them gave her biblical advice, rather they offered her an opinion based on the world's stance. This must truly break God's heart.

If you're called upon to be a mentor, how will you represent truth?

Let's close with one last principle from our passage. What did Paul tell us to do with what we've learned from him **(Philippians 4:9)**?

Explain further using **James 1:22-25**.

I believe a believer's joy (or lack thereof) is directly related to Paul's message in Philippians and this passage in James. Just reading the Word of God won't do anything for us. But if we meditate on it and live by it, then it penetrates the deep crevices of our heart and washes away all the dirt. It surely revives our soul **(Psalm 19:7)**. So what will you do with this?

Ponder the *Finding Fullness of Joy* principle and then write it at the back of the book.

Finding Fullness of Joy

Take captive every thought and renew your mind with truth.

Day 4
Learning to be Content

Joyous Jewel

I have learned to be content whatever the circumstances. Philippians 4:11

Contentment is a sense of satisfaction – an ease of mind – and we often think it's somehow related to how good our circumstances are, the things we've accomplished, or the stuff we've accumulated. When our health is good, our kids are happy and successful, we're paying the bills with a little left over at the end of the month, our car is working and running, our ministry is flourishing, our bank account is expanding, and we're getting along with others; we sit back and thank God for His blessings and provisions. Most of us have at one time or another felt contentment, but it usually doesn't last long because trials are inevitable, and they always show up when we're least expecting them. It's a known fact that struggles can push contentment right out the door of our peaceful heart.

On the other hand, the apostle Paul wants to tell us about another kind of contentment – a contentment that *is* possible when things aren't going so well. A contentment that can last when life is turned upside down. Of course, the world doesn't understand this kind of contentment, but believers in Christ can know it. True contentment, as Paul would call it, is when we can… rejoice with someone's success without being jealous, look for and celebrate the little steps forward, use the gifts God has given to us rather than comparing ours with others, move forward without competing for others' approval, stay positive in the midst of negativity, and enjoy what we have rather than get restless.

I know I want this kind of contentment. I think you do too. Here's the thing… if Paul can be content, then we can too.

Write down the theme of **Philippians 4:10-13**. Be sure to record the principles.

The apostle Paul is about to lead us on a journey to finding true contentment. From our passage, I would like to pull out three principles that can help us achieve this kind of contentment. Spend quality time on each one, learning from the apostle who found it.

Contentment is found by…

Staying connected to God's people!

According to **Philippians 4:10**, why were the Philippian believers so important to Paul?

Now, read **Philippians 4:14-18** and explain what Paul was talking about when he said, **"I rejoice greatly in the Lord that at last you have renewed your concern for me"** (Philippians 4:10).

According to **1 Corinthians 9:14**, how was the Philippian church fulfilling their God-given command?

Through the centuries, most Christians serving the Lord full-time have been underpaid. They often work harder and labor longer than normal lay people in the church. Some have sacrificed greatly for the work of the Lord. Certainly, in today's mega-church culture there are some who do very well, but a great majority live meagerly and depend on God's people to help meet their basic needs. For most of them, that's perfectly fine. They have a healthy attitude about money and they are pastoring, leading, evangelizing, and teaching out of devotion to Jesus Christ and a love for His people. Still, it's biblically correct for the church to aid them in their work. We will examine giving in more detail in our final lesson, but it's obvious Paul felt extreme gratitude for the way the Philippians helped him, not because of the monetary gift but because of their partnership in spreading the gospel.

Based on the following Scriptures, what does staying connected to God's people produce?

1 Thessalonians 2:19-20:

Philemon 1:7:

Imagine the look on Paul's face when Epaphroditus showed up, having traveled approximately 800 miles to deliver a gift. In our high tech and instant world, we cannot fathom that. But something tells me that from the moment he left Philippi, Epaphroditus was envisioning a grand reunion with his special friend. Oh, the amount of joy it brought to both of them. I imagine that for Paul, Epaphroditus' visit was like hearing the cheers in the crowd that kept him pressing on. It refreshed his spirit, inspired his vision, and validated his ministry. What a blessing it is to be connected to God's people.

Are you connected to God's people? Are you learning beside others? Serving next to Christians brothers or sisters? Praying with other prayer warriors? Write down what staying connected to God's people has done for you. If you're not connected, how will you get connected?

Resting in God's provision!

What do you learn about contentment in **Philippians 4:11**?

The prophet Isaiah gives a beautiful description of how to attain contentment in **Isaiah 55:1-2**. Using these verses, explain how contentment is found.

It's interesting to know that contentment doesn't come naturally for any of us. Paul had to learn it. We must too. But seeking after Jesus is one sure way to finally be content in any situation. As we spend time getting to know Christ, He will surely become more important than anything. In his song, *More Than Enough,* Chris Tomlin sings: "All of you is more than enough for all of me. For every thirst and every need You satisfy me with Your love. And all I have in You is more than enough." [6] We might sum up this point by saying that contentment doesn't come from what we have, but from WHOM we have.

What does Paul tell you about himself, according to **Philippians 4:12**?

Paul knew from the beginning his ministry would not be easy. Jesus said, **"I will show him how much he must suffer for my name" (Acts 9:16)**. And he suffered greatly. We often get upset when our air conditioning goes out, when the Internet fails, or when our car is broken. I remember a pastor getting upset and harshly reprimanding a staff member because the water in the baptismal tank was cold after the power had gone out the night before. In Paul's day, they didn't have baptismal tanks with warm water. They baptized people in the freezing cold river.

Paul was writing from a prison cell in Rome. If he had measured contentment by his good circumstances, he would have never found it. We surely cannot understand the kinds of inconveniences or hardships Paul went through, but he accepted the good with the bad. Paul was content no matter what.

What is the command in **Hebrews 13:5**?

Why is contentment possible for the believer based on **2 Peter 1:3**?

What does Paul write to Timothy in **1 Timothy 6:6-7**?

Paul saw God's provision and he became perfectly content in that provision. He had learned contentment and then tells Timothy that contentment is great gain. Why do you think it's a gain?

Well, contentment seems to alleviate stress, anxiety, jealousy, worry, and restlessness. When God becomes enough for us, then we don't long for satisfaction in other places.

Have you learned to be content in any situation? Write down your thoughts.

Contentment is found by...

Drawing from God's strength!

Write out **Philippians 4:13**.

What do you think this verse means within the context of **Philippians 4:11-13**?

Where does our strength come from?

Philippians 4:13 is one of the most quoted Scriptures in the Bible. But today we need to look at it within the context of **Philippians 4** and finding contentment. The Greek word for *strength* means, "to make strong, inwardly strengthen." I believe Paul is saying that contentment *is* possible because of the strength that Jesus puts in us. Perhaps this was the secret he was talking about in **verse 12**.

So if Jesus puts strength in all of His people, why do you think some are discontented?

I do believe that a great majority of Christians are not operating in the strength God has given to them. If they were, then we would see less division, bickering, and drifting within the church. I don't know about you, but I want to experience His strength so much more in my life. I long to have the same kind of contentment, devotion, and impact that Paul had. I believe Paul wanted it for the people of Philippi, too. To do this, you and I need to draw from it. Paul has been setting the stage for us to find contentment. Go back and review the week's lessons. What principles do you believe will help you in drawing strength – the strength already in you?

Examine the *Finding Fullness of Joy* principle and then write it at the back of the book.

Finding Fullness of Joy

Operating in God's strength to be content in every situation.

Day 5
Beautiful Offerings

Joyous Jewel

They are a fragrant offering, an acceptable sacrifice pleasing to God.
Philippians 4:18

Today we conclude our Bible study on Philippians, a bittersweet moment for me. I loved the apostle Paul before I began this journey, but my love and admiration has just grown over the past six weeks. I love Paul's transparency, his humble spirit, his love for God's people, his devotion to truth, and his allegiance to Jesus. He surely set the bar high for those of us who have come behind him. For centuries, no doubt, he has been enjoying sweet fellowship with the One who offered him a brand-new life. I can't wait to meet him.

On our final day together, we end on a beautiful topic: *offerings*. It may just change our perspective on how we look at giving and the church. Did you know that the Bible references money and possessions more than Jesus talked about love, heaven and hell combined? That's crazy. There are many reasons why the Bible talks about money, but today we cover a wonderful aspect: partnership in the gospel. And Paul will commend the Philippian church for their part. How they must have smiled when the final section of Paul's letter was read.

The passage before us today is not really about money, though some could take it that way. It's really about *generosity*. Generosity is giving freely and from the abundance of your heart. Paul will show us how the Philippian church is an example for the body of Christ in generosity.

Read **Philippians 4:14-23**. Highlight the things about the Philippian church that stand out to you. What do you learn about generosity?

From this passage, let me draw out four specific benefits that stem from generosity:

Generosity is good!

What did Paul say to the church at Philippi in **Philippians 4:14-15**?

Does this give you any idea of why this church was so special to Paul? Explain.

134

Philippi was in the province of Macedonia. What do you learn about the churches in Macedonia from **2 Corinthians 8:1-5**?

People might assume the church at Philippi was a wealthy church, but this passage tells us differently. They gave from what they didn't have. And sometimes they were all alone in their giving to Paul. Why would they do this? Because they believed in Paul's mission and they also wanted to help him accomplish the work of the Lord. They had the comforts of being connected to a church family, food on the table, and a bed to sleep in at night. They knew that Paul didn't always have those things. He was on the front lines serving God with very little. He surely couldn't have moved forward without the help of this generous church.

What is the lesson in **Mark 12:41-44**?

Imagine the smile on Jesus' face when He witnessed this generous offering by this widow. Now imagine the smile on His face when we give to His work from what we don't have. There are many people like the rich ones in this story (and God honors their giving), but few like the poor widow. We should always give to God's work. It's more than okay to give to ministries outside the local church – ministries that are on mission with Jesus. We need to pray about the ministry God would have us give to because giving progresses God's work.

Is God asking you to give today? What is He speaking to you about?

Generosity reaps rewards!

Why was Paul thankful for the gifts the church sent to him **(Philippians 4:17)**?

The apostle Paul wasn't looking at the gifts for what would benefit him, but what would benefit the church. The word *credited* was a term used in the money-markets of the day, namely, "interest which may accumulate to their account." [8] Imagine that! Their generosity was an investment worth every penny. It would repay rich dividends. Their partnership with Paul gave him the opportunity to continue to preach the Good News, write letters, start churches, and disciple believers. And you and I, in the 21st century, are reaping what the Philippian church sowed into Paul.

Pastors and leaders who run churches usually have the church folk, and maybe a denominational organization, to help them. But parachurch ministries – those serving outside the local church – rely on generous givers to help them. Many are supported by donations. I must admit that I'm very thankful for those who have given to Solid Truth Ministries. I do not do what I do for money and sometimes I have just enough to do the next project. But anyone who gives to this ministry is partnering with me in empowering believers in solid truth. Their investment will surely reap great benefits on earth and in heaven.

Ponder **Proverbs 11:25**. What is God saying to you right now?

What does **Luke 6:38** mean to you regarding being generous?

Generosity is pleasing to God!

What is a generous offering to God **(Philippians 4:18)**?

The believers would understand this phrase **"a fragrant offering, an acceptable sacrifice,"** as an Old Testament phrase. When the priests in the temple offered an acceptable sacrifice, the Bible tells us that **"it [was] an aroma pleasing to the LORD" (Leviticus 1:9)**. Hence, God is pleased with sacrificial gifts. There are certain smells that stop me in my tracks and I can't help but to breathe them in. The same with God. When we sacrificially give from the generous part of our heart, the smell reaches Him, and He breathes it in until He is well pleased. I picture Him going, "Ah. Such a beautiful smell."

There is nothing more important to me than to know I've pleased my God. How about you? Do you want to please God? Write out your prayer asking God to show what you can do to please Him. *Then make sure to follow through with God's direction.

What is the result of such a fragrant offering, according to **Philippians 4:19**?

I'm sure you realize this verse has been taken out of context a whole lot. People often claim this verse and then run with it, without giving serious consideration to the whole context. These words come on the heels of generosity – giving to God's people. Did you notice this verse says, "God will meet all your *needs*?" Not your wants, but your needs. This is one benefit God gives to those who offer sweet-smelling sacrifices.

What is the principle and the result of obedience in **Proverbs 3:9-10**?

Generosity aids in spreading the work of God!

How far-reaching was Paul's ministry **(Philippians 4:21-23)**?

In referencing this passage, Pastor Skip Heitzig said that the "goers" and the "senders" are partners. Both are equal ambassadors in Christ's work. I love that Paul mentioned the believers in Caesar's household. By saying this, he was telling the church that their generosity allowed him the opportunity to spread the Good News to the world and many Roman elite came to Christ. This must have brought such joy to their hearts.

God is always faithful to His people. You and I may not be called to serve on the mission field, reach the unreached in remote areas, or lead a para-church ministry, but we can partner with those who are by generously aiding them in their efforts. In God's eyes, this is a truly acceptable offering because it allows God's work to go around the world.

I must say this, though: there are many ministries that do not have God's best interest at hand. They are driven by impure motives. So, we must choose wisely. For instance, one of my favorite pastors is Skip Heitzig from Calvary Church in Albuquerque, New Mexico. I have learned a great deal from his biblically-sound teachings. So one day I went on their website and gave a donation. I felt God telling me to do that. We must be very careful, though, because we want our gift to go to a ministry that will further the kingdom of God, not hinder it.

What is God speaking to you about today? What will you do?

I trust this Bible study has helped you attain fuller joy. I hope you have gleaned amazing truths from this little, but powerful book. Make sure to review the *Finding Fullness of Joy* principles periodically as they will help you to keep pressing on with joy. Keep your eyes on the finish line because it's not too far off. And always stay focused on God's Word.

Write down any final thoughts before writing the *Finding Fullness of Joy* principle at the back of the book.

Finding Fullness of Joy

Being generous with your resources

1. https://www.biblestudytools.com/lexicons/greek/nas/merimnao.html

2. https://www.studylight.org/language-studies/greek-thoughts.html?article=35

3. LOGOS, *Wuest's Word Studies in the Greek New Testament*.

4. Warren Wiersbe, *Be Joyful*, (Colorado Springs, CO: David C. Cook), p. 132.

5. ibid, p. 132.

6.https://www.google.com/search?q=enough+lyrics+by+chris+tomlin&rlz=1C1CHBF_enUS776 US776&oq=enough+lyrics+by+chris+tomlin&aqs=chrome..69i57j0l5.7422j0j4&sourceid=chro me&ie=UTF-8

7. W. E. Vine, *Vines Complete Expository Dictionary* (Nashville, TN: Thomas Nelson, Inc.), 198.

8. LOGOS, *Wuest's Word Studies in the Greek New Testament*.

Finding Fullness of Joy Principles

Week 1

Day 1 _____

Day 2 _____

Day 3 _____

Day 4 _____

Day 5 _____

Week 2

Day 1 _____

Day 2 _____

Day 3 _____

Day 4 _____

Day 5 _____

Week 3

Day 1 _____

Day 2 _____

Day 3 _____

Day 4 _____

Day 5 _____

Week 4

Day 1 _____

Day 2 _____

Day 3 _____

Day 4 _____

Day 5 _____

Week 5

Day 1 _____

Day 2 _____

Day 3 _____

Day 4 _____

Day 5 _____

Week 6

Day 1 _____

Day 2 _____

Day 3 _____

Day 4 _____

Day 5 _____

Weekly Discussion Questions

Week 1 – Paul and the Beloved Philippians

Day 1: Looking at Paul and Silas in prison, how should we respond in not-so-good situations? How would you describe Lydia? In what ways should we emulate her?

Day 2: What does the term bond-servant mean to you? How can we be bond-servants of Jesus? What made the church of Philippi so special to Paul? Discuss each thing.

Day 3: Based on Paul's prayer, what should we seek in our walk with Christ? Why are these things important? What are some specific ways we can pray for other believers?

Day 4: What was Paul's passion? Why? Discuss how Paul used his place of confinement. How did God use Paul's situation for the good? Does God still work this way?

Day 5: How did Paul handle those with impure motives? How can we get past those causing us trouble?

Week 2 – All for Christ

Day 1: How can we expect God's outcome in every situation, good or bad? In what ways did the apostle Paul live with a heavenly perspective? How can we?

Day 2: What did you learn about heaven? How do these things change your perspective about life? Why is heaven better? What is one thing you're excited about heaven?

Day 3: Revisit 1 Timothy 4:12-15 and pick out some of the ways we can progress in our Christian life.

Day 4: How can we become good representatives of the kingdom of God? How does being a good representative help us to stand against opposers? How can we stand firm?

Day 5: In what venues have you seen persecution? How have you witnessed it? What is a godly response to persecution?

Week 3 – To Please God

Day 1: How have you witnessed disunity in the church, the family, the world? What is the result of disunity? What can we do to bring unity in our sphere of influence?

Day 2: Describe the self-generation we live in. Is it good or bad? What can we do to not be a part of the selfie generation?

Day 3: How can we imitate Jesus' attitude? How does our attitude determine whether we have joy or not?

Day 4: Discuss each exalted position of Jesus. What does Jesus' exalted position mean for you?

Day 5: Why is it important we work out our salvation? How can we do this successfully?

Week 4 – Sweet Smelling Sacrifices

Day 1: How does complaining and arguing hinder our witness? The world is bent and twisted, but the believer is supposed to walk straight. How can we do this?

Day 2: Describe someone who has poured his life into yours? What do you admire the most about this person? In what ways can we pour ourselves in someone?

Day 3: How did Timothy add to Paul's joy? Describe a like-minded person. Why are those the kinds of people we need by our side?

Day 4: What makes Epaphroditus such a valued partner to the apostle Paul? Do you have someone like him in your life? What value do these kinds of people offer?

Day 5: What is the difference between a servant of the world and a servant of Jesus? How can we attain a servant heart?

Week 5 – Admirable Ambition

Day 1: Discuss why joy is an anchor and a safeguard for us. How can we be like the Judaizers in today's world?

Day 2: What credentials do we sometimes gloat about? What inspires you about the apostle Paul – after his conversion? Where does our confidence belong?

Day 3: What did Paul seek after above everything else? How do you see this in his life? What are you seeking after more than anything else?

Day 4: Discuss the race. Is it easy? Is there a finish line? How was Paul able to keep running despite his circumstances? How can we press on as well?

Day 5: What are you most excited about heaven? How can thoughts of heaven keep us in the race and can give us the stamina to keep running?

Week 6 – Peace and Contentment

Day 1: How can the church be a haven for the hurting, the wounded, and the lost? What are some things we can do to restore relationships?

Day 2: Do you think that most people deal with anxiety? What is your answer based on? What principles did you gain from Philippians 4:6-7 that can help set us free from anxiety?

Day 3: How have your thoughts played a role in your actions? Give an illustration. Discuss the four principles that can help us conquer negative thoughts.

Day 4: What does contentment look like in the middle of not-so-good circumstances? Is it even possible? How do you know?

Day 5: Does God honor generosity? Answer using Philippians 4:14-23. How can we follow the example of the Philippian church?

Favorite Biblical Resources

Bible Dictionaries
Vines Complete Expository Dictionary
Holman Bible Dictionary
The Revell Bible Dictionary
Smith's Bible Dictionary
Unger's Bible Dictionary

Bible Concordances
Strong's Exhaustive Concordance of the Bible
Zondervan NIV Exhaustive Concordance

Bible Commentaries
"Be" Series by Warren Wiersbe
J. Vernon McGee Series
Matthew Henry Complete Bible Commentary

Reputable Authors
Warren Wiersbe
Howard Hendricks
Kay Arthur
Charles Spurgeon
Charles Swindoll
David Jeremiah
Billy Graham

About the Author

There is nothing that gives me greater joy than to watch God open peoples' hearts to the truth of His Word. Words cannot describe the joy in my heart every time I hear what God is doing in the lives of His people through one of our Bible studies. Sometimes I think I can hear heaven's hosts shouting *Halleluiah*.

Joy is something God promises to believers. This gift *is* possible no matter what's going on in our lives. Yet, many people struggle to find fullness of joy. I've been there. But the good news is that God has given us a resource to help us attain joy. And that source is the book of Philippians. I believe this Bible study will be a wonderful tool to help us gain what God has promised us. Blessings to you as you learn from Paul, one of the most beloved apostles and the greatest evangelist of the first century.

Thank you for taking this journey with me.

In Him,

Sheryl

Sheryl Pellatiro is an active Bible study teacher, author, and speaker. Her website (www.solidtruthministries.com) hosts many of her Bible teachings. You can email Sheryl at: sheryl@solidtruthministries.com.

Other Bible Studies

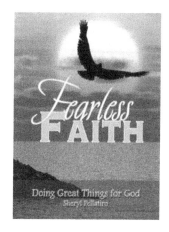

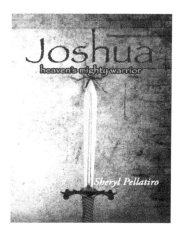

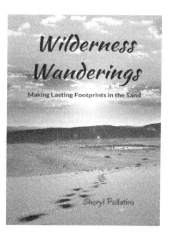

Visit our website for more resources, to sign up for our e-newsletter, and/or to receive all the latest up-to-date happenings with the ministry:

www.solidtruthministries.com

We are a ministry committed to equipping believers in the Word of God through Bible study materials, Bible study classes (both locally and nationally), online Bible classes, leadership workshops, conferences, blogs, and many other venues.

Our Mission...

To build up God's people on a firm foundation.

Our Focus...

To come along side you, pray for you, and encourage you through the many biblical resources God has given to us that will help you draw closer to Him. This ministry is designed to energize your current relationship and walk with our Lord, or perhaps assist you in beginning a new walk with Him. We are here for you.

Our Vision...

To strengthen and empower believers globally with solid truth and equip them with life skills for their family and community. Another vision is to bring the truth of God's Word to those who may be questioning what they believe.

Please help us take the message of God's Word into your community.

Evaluation Form

After completing the Bible study, please take a moment to complete the evaluation form and send it to:

sheryl@solidtruthministries.com

Bible Study Complete: _____

Your Information:

Name: _____

Address: _____

City: _____ State: _____ Zip: _____

Email Address: _____

Yes, please include me on your e-newsletter list* _____

Church Information:

Church Name: _____

Address: _____

City: _____ State: _____ Zip: _____

What did you enjoy the most about the Bible study?

What did you struggle with the most?

What insight(s) did you receive?

Did you complete the study in a class setting or on your own?

Please submit any testimonials, comments or suggestions.

*Solid Truth Ministries, Inc. does not sell our mailing lists to outside sources. All information is collected and used for the sole purpose of informing you about any and all activities relating to Solid Truth Ministries, Inc.

31954163R00086

Made in the USA
Middletown, DE
03 January 2019